Caligula & Nero: Rome's Worst Emperors

By Charles River Editors

A Roman coin from 38 A.D. depicting Caligula

# About Charles River Editors

**Charles River Editors** was founded by Harvard and MIT alumni to provide superior editing and original writing services, with the expertise to create digital content for publishers across a vast range of subject matter. In addition to providing original digital content for third party publishers, Charles River Editors republishes civilization's greatest literary works, bringing them to a new generation via ebooks.

# Introduction

**Bust of Caligula**

## Caligula (12-41 A.D.)

"He seldom had anyone put to death except by numerous slight wounds, his constant order, which soon became well-known, being: 'Strike so that he may feel that he is dying.' When a different man than he had intended had been killed, through a mistake in the names, he said that the victim too had deserved the same fate. He often uttered the familiar line of the tragic poet: 'Let them hate me, so they but fear me.'"– Suetonius, *Lives of the Twelve Caesars*

Throughout the history of the Roman Empire, many rulers held the reins of ultimate power. Some of them, like Octavian, Trajan, Hadrian, Constantine, and Marcus Aurelius, are still celebrated and considered among antiquity's great statesmen, generals and thinkers. But the Roman Empire also had its fair share of notorious villains, from the sadistic Nero to the debauched Commodus. And yet, all of Rome's poor rulers pale in comparison to the record and legacy of Gaius Julius Caesar Augustus Germanicus, a young man remembered by posterity as Caligula.

Given how bad some of Rome's emperors were, it's a testament to just how insane and reviled Caligula was that he is still remembered nearly 2,000 years later as the epitome of everything that could be wrong with a tyrant. The Romans had high hopes for him after he succeeded Tiberius in 37 A.D., and by all accounts he was a noble and just ruler during his first few months in power. But after that, he suffered some sort of mysterious illness that apparently rendered him insane. Indeed, the list of Caligula's strange actions is long. Among other things, Caligula began appearing in public dressed as gods and goddesses, and his incest, sexual perversion, and thirst for blood were legendary at the time, difficult accomplishments considering Roman society was fairly accustomed to and tolerant of such things.

In fact, the Romans were so taken aback by some of Caligula's behavior that historians catalogued some of his strangest antics. Suetonius wrote that as Caligula's relationship with the Senate deteriorated, he ordered that Incitatus be made a member of the Roman Senate and a Consul. Incitatus, Latin for "swift," was Caligula's favorite horse. But far from simply being a way to stick it to the Senate, Caligula invited guests to dine with Incitatus and had the horse's stables made of marble, suggesting Caligula was simply mentally unstable himself.

Caligula has always fascinated people, and people have speculated for centuries whether the stories about his misdeeds are true. What is clear is that the Romans had more than enough by 41 A.D., when the Praetorian Guard turned on the young emperor and assassinated him. Caligula's reign was so traumatic to the Romans that they even considered restoring the Republic, but military officials ultimately installed Claudius, the only male left in the Julian family line, as emperor.

*Caligula & Nero* chronicles the life, stories, and legacy of the famous Roman emperor. Along with pictures of art depicting important people and places, as well as a bibliography and Table of Contents, you will learn about Caligula like never before.

## Nero (37-68 A.D.)

"What an artist dies with me!" – Attributed to Nero just before his suicide

Throughout the annals of history, there have been few figures as reviled as Lucius Domitius Ahenobarbus, better known as Nero Claudius Caesar Drusus Germanicus, or more simply, Nero. Even today, he remains one of the Roman Empire's most famous – or notorious – figures, a villain whose impact on popular culture is so vast that his name crops up consistently to this day in literature, film, TV and mediums as unlikely as video games and anime.

Nero ranks among the very worst of the Caesars, alongside the likes of mad Caligula, slothful Commodus, and paranoid Domitian, a figure so hated that, in many ancient Christian traditions, he is literally, without hyperbole, considered the Antichrist; according to a notable Biblical scholar, the coming of the Beast and the number 666 in the Book of Revelation are references to Nero. He was the man who, famously, "fiddled while Rome burned", an inveterate lecher, a murderous tyrant who showed little compunction in murdering his mother and who liked to use Christian martyrs as a source of illumination at night – by burning them alive. His economic policies, according to many historians, virtually bankrupted Rome.

Even his appearance, apparently, was ill-favoured. His busts show him to be fleshy-faced, with a weak chin that he attempted to disguise with a distinctly unprepossessing beard, and according to Suetionius he was also spotty, stinking, pot-bellied and thin-legged – not a pretty picture.

The best known accounts of Nero come from biographers like Tacitus, Cassius Dio, Suetionius and Josephus, but there are also indications that, to some extent, reports of Nero's cruelty were exaggerated. Nero was popular with the common people and much of the army, and during his reign the Empire enjoyed a period of remarkable peace and stability. Many historians, including some of his ancient biographers – such as Josephus – suggest that there existed a strong bias against Nero. Part of this is because his successors wished to discredit him, and justify the insurrections which eventually drove him, hounded from the throne, to a lonely suicide. Much of the bias against Nero can also be attributed to the fact that he was a renowned persecutor of Christians, and since many of the historians who wrote about Nero in the years after his death were Christians themselves, it made sense for them to have a jaundiced view of their erstwhile nemesis. Because of this, some historians have suggested that Nero's demeanour and reputation might not be as black as the original sources might be inclined to suggest.

*Caligula & Nero* looks at the life of one of Rome's most notorious emperors and attempts to separate fact from fiction to analyze his reign and legacy. Along with pictures of important people, places, and events, you will learn about Nero like never before.

Coin showing Nero donating money to a citizen, circa 64-66 A.D.

# Caligula

### Chapter 1: Caligula's Early Years

"Safe is Rome, safe too our country, for Germanicus is safe."

Gaius Julius Caesar Augustus Germanicus, named in honor of Julius Caesar and his own father, was born into one of the noblest families in the Roman Empire on August 31, 12 A.D. His father, Germanicus Julius Caesar, was closely related to both Augustus and Mark Antony. Germanicus was a highly honorable and successful general who had a fairly decent claim to the position of Emperor, but he had chosen to abide by Augustus's decision and support Tiberius instead. Caligula's mother was Vipsania Agrippina, better known as Agrippina the Elder, also a direct descendant of Augustus. Agrippina the Elder was related to Tiberius and the future emperor Claudius by marriage.

**Marble bust of Germanicus**

**Bust of Agrippina the Elder**

Both of Caligula's parents were remembered by their contemporaries with adoration, and there is little indication that they neglected Gaius as a young boy. In fact, Caligula's nickname came from the fact that he had accompanied his father on military campaign. When the boy was only two years old, Germanicus had Gaius travel with his legions to Germania, a privilege that his two older children, Drusus and Nero Germanicus, were apparently not afforded. Germanicus had been given the command of eight legions, but it was also an extremely risky venture to undertake any sort of campaign across the Rhine, as the Germanic tribesmen had shown themselves to be by far the most vicious and dangerous enemies of Rome. In 9 A.D., only 5 years before Germanicus was posted to Germania, four legions under Quinctilius Varus had been surprised by Germanic warriors during their march into the Teutoburg Forest and were completely massacred, a loss of almost 20,000 men that was possibly the greatest disaster in Roman military history. But Germanicus was not a man to be threatened by even the gravest of dangers, and he was so confident of success that he brought his toddler and his wife with him, a highly unorthodox move that raised eyebrows among the Roman ruling elite. The Romans didn't think an armed camp was a place for a woman of noble patrician stock.

Despite Germanicus's confidence, the campaign was fraught with peril, and the first threat came not from the Germans but from his own men. When he reached the legions in their encampment in 14 A.D., he found the men in an uproar and close to open mutiny. They had been initially promised their enlistments would be downgraded from 20 years to 16, only to find that the emperor Tiberius had reneged on his promise. For strategic reasons, Tiberius had decided to force them to abide by their original two-decade terms of service. The infuriated legionaries called for the newly arrived Germanicus to declare himself Emperor, and pledged him their support. However, Germanicus chose to be loyal to Tiberius and ordered the ringleaders of the attempted mutiny to be arrested and put to death, thus proving to the suspicious Emperor that he was a faithful servant who could be fully trusted with independent command.

**Bust of Tiberius**

At the same time, Germanicus realized his display of loyalty had earned him the dislike of his men. Knowing that only victory could make them happy, he led them in a lightning campaign across the Rhine against the Marsi, most of whom he exterminated or enslaved. Since Germanicus led from the front and Agrippina did not wish to be separated from him, it is likely that Gaius himself would have been close at hand for much of the campaign; if he was not on the field of battle itself, he was certainly very close to it.

Germanicus retired to winter quarters, only to strike again the following year. This time he marched into the very heart of Germania against a coalition that had freed itself from servitude to

Rome and had massacred the legions in Teutoburg Forest, taking four eagles in the process. Although his desires to fight a war of attrition that would wipe out the Germanic armies were largely frustrated by his inability to bring Arminius and his men to decisive battle, Germanicus was able to capture Arminius's wife Thusnelda. Somewhat to the chagrin of Agrippina, Thusnelda was permitted to share Germanicus's quarters as a mark of respect, an indication that he was more interested in a stable conquest than punitive raids.

Germanicus vowed to avenge the men who had fallen at the Battle of the Teutoburg Forest, and the following year, after having visited the forest and laid the bones of the fallen which still littered the ground to rest, he launched an attack against Arminius's strongholds. Although his advance guard very nearly fell into the same trap that had annihilated Varus's legions, Germanicus was able to emerge victorious before the coming of winter forced him back to his encampments. The following spring, in 16 A.D., despite the fact that the cautious Tiberius had warned him against such a move, Germanicus renewed his assault with fresh levies at his command, once again bringing Agrippina and Gaius with him. After years of provocation, Germanicus was at last successful in goading Arminius and his coalition into open battle along the Weser River. On the banks of the river, a force of 8 Roman legions and approximately 30,000 auxiliaries faced an army of 50,000 Germanic tribesmen. After a harrowing day's fighting, Germanicus drove Arminius's men from the field with a loss of over 20,000 men, while the Romans and their auxiliaries had lost only around 1,000 soldiers. Winter once again forced Germanicus back to the Rhine, but the following year he was able to launch another successful campaign, this time recovering several of the eagles that had been lost at the Teutoburg Forest.

Germanicus's military success made him exceedingly popular with his troops, but it did not endear him to Tiberius. Jealous of the general's high standing with the people, Tiberius recalled Germanicus from the Rhine, promising him a triumph as a way of softening the blow of his removal from command, which was explained away as being necessary because Germanicus had exceeded his orders by carrying the war so often across the Rhine.

Obedient to the imperial summons, Germanicus left his legions behind and set off for Rome with Agrippina and Gaius in tow. His family now also included Agrippina the Younger (born in 15 A.D.) and Julia Drusilla (born 16 A.D.). For 4 year old Gaius, the change was probably an unwelcome one. By all accounts, he had been spoiled by the soldiers in camp, and they were the ones who had first bestowed the nickname "Caligula" upon him. The affectionate term sprang from Germanicus's choice to have the young boy dressed up in a miniature version of full military regalia, right down to baby-sized *caligae*, the tough infantryman's boots. Being extremely taken with this, the soldiers took to calling him Caligula, meaning "little *caligae*", or "little sandals", and the nickname has remained with him ever since. For his part, Caligula was never fond of the nickname, and it was almost certainly never said to his face when he grew older. That's no surprise, given that it would've been a grave breach of form to call even the most benevolent ruler "little sandals", and it would have been a fatal mistake to say it to a man as unstable as Caligula.

**A caliga. Picture taken by Matthias Kabel.**

After his triumph, where he was acclaimed by the crowd with a fervor far surpassing what they reserved for the gloomy Tiberius himself, Germanicus was quickly dispatched to Asia. Once again, he elected to take his entire family with him, other than Caligula's two older brothers. While Germanicus was in Asia Minor, Agrippina the Elder added another child to the family (Julia Livilla, born in 18 A.D.), and he quickly proved that his military exploits were no flash in the pan. In a lightning campaign, he annexed Cappadocia and Commagene, adding them to the empire. However, while he was on a visit to Egypt in 19 A.D., it appears Germanicus caused Tiberius severe offense and great concern by apparently behaving in a manner more fitting of an emperor than a mere general. Germanicus then worsened his situation by getting into a spat with Gnaeus Piso, a provincial governor who had interfered with the arrangements Germanicus had established for his newly conquered domains. Germanicus ordered Piso back to Rome, which greatly angered Tiberius because he had no official right to do so. Shortly thereafter, Germanicus died mysteriously in Antioch. All indications are that he was poisoned by someone under orders from Piso, who in turn was receiving his commands from Tiberius himself. The theory that Tiberius was involved is made all the more probable by the fact that Piso himself died mysteriously just before he was due to give evidence in the matter of Germanicus's death.

With Germanicus dead, Agrippina and her children were adrift in the world. However, she had proven herself a strong and resourceful woman, and she had already raised a number of eyebrows in Germania by issuing orders and demanding obedience in her husband's name when he was away. She returned to Rome with Caligula and her daughters, taking up residence on the

Palatine Hill in 19 A.D., where she continued to raise her family with the help of Germanicus's mother. She also became enmeshed in the politics of the imperial court, working as a strident advocate for her own children to take precedence in the imperial succession over Tiberius's illegitimate son, Tiberius Gemellus.

Agrippina's stance, though it was ultimately successful, did little to endear her to Tiberius, who became increasingly hostile towards her. To be fair, it should be noted that he had become increasingly hostile to everyone during the time, but in 26 A.D., Tiberius refused Agrippina's request to let her remarry. He rejected her wishes either because he was afraid of a powerful union or out of spiteful revenge based on her opposition to the Praetorian Guard faction led by his favorite, Sejanus. Some time later, Tiberius allegedly tried to poison Agrippina with an apple, causing mutual resentment between the two to become all-out hatred.

In 29 A.D., matters came to a head when Agrippina and Caligula's brothers were arrested on Tiberius's orders and brought before the Senate on trumped-up charges. Agrippina was banished to Pandataria (Ventotene), a remote Mediterranean island, while Nero Germanicus was sent to the island of Ponza. Nero Germanicus died mysteriously a short time later, either as an induced suicide or because he was literally starved to death.

Caligula was spared the emperor's wrath by virtue of the fact he was only 17 and thus not yet a man. He may have been too young to be punished, but he was not too young to learn hate. He was sent to live with Augustus's widow Livia, his great-grandmother. Livia was a woman with a political mind as keen as a razor, and she almost unquestionably left her mark on Caligula before she died, after which Caligula's guardianship was taken over by his grandmother Antonia.

In 31 A.D., Tiberius's paranoia reached a new peak following his orchestrated assassination of Sejanus, whom he suspected of plotting against him. He ordered Caligula to become his personal ward on the island of Capri, in order to keep a closer eye on him. At this point, all that Caligula had left in the world were his sisters, but Tiberius deprived him of them as well. Caligula likely hated Tiberius, but he was wise enough to conceal his animosity and behaved towards the emperor with virtually shameless devotion and loyalty in public. All the while, Caligula was secretly plotting the emperor's downfall.

Trapped within the tiny (albeit beautiful) confines of the island of Capri, separated from his family, and with his mother and brother languishing in prison, Caligula must undoubtedly have nurtured a deep resentment. That Caligula managed to publicly conceal his hatred in 33 A.D. is truly remarkable. That year, Agrippina the Elder was flogged on Tiberius's orders by one of her guardsmen, losing an eye in the process, and his brother Drusus starved to death in his cell. Drusus was so hungry that he gnawed on his own bedding in his final agony. Shortly thereafter, despite being force-fed food, Agrippina also starved to death, though it is also possible that Tiberius starved her as he did Drusus (and possibly Nero Germanicus). Caligula and his sisters were now alone in the world.

According to a story he recounted later, Caligula allegedly slipped into Tiberius's bedroom one night, armed with a knife, but lost his nerve and dropped it on the floor. According to Caligula, Tiberius caught him in the act but never mentioned the incident, making the whole affair rather dubious. Even if the story isn't true, it demonstrates how Caligula felt about Tiberius at the time, and understandably so.

Possibly as a way of making amends for the deaths of his mother and brothers, Tiberius made Caligula a *quaestor* in 33 A.D. and also arranged a marriage for him with Junia Claudilla. However, he was given no formal powers as quaestor, and Junia died during childbirth a few months later. During this time, Caligula began to appreciate that his future in the deadly world of Roman politics would require a more mature outlook, and he began to cultivate an acquaintance with Naevius Macro, Prefect of the Praetorian Guard and a vastly influential man who also had Tiberius's ear. This likely helped raise Caligula's standing with the emperor. Two years later, possibly as a result of Macro's machinations, Caligula was named heir to Tiberius's estate along with his illegitimate son Tiberius Gemellus. Despite their ugly history, Tiberius actually came to favor Caligula as his heir, likely because he suspected that Gemellus was actually Sejanus's illegitimate son rather than his own.

In 37 AD, Tiberius died suddenly. Although he was in his late 70s at the time, he had appeared healthy before suddenly taking ill. While a sudden death would not necessarily mean there was foul play, the fact that he was almost universally hated at this point makes the circumstances of his death mysterious. According to some ancient sources, Macro smothered Tiberius in his bed with a pillow once he was certain the Emperor had named Caligula as his successor, while some place the blame on Caligula himself. In *I, Claudius*, Caligula is depicted as being the one who smothers Tiberius, only to fail to kill him in the first attempt and thus having to do it all over again.

Either way, as soon as Tiberius was dead, Caligula acted quickly. With Macro's support, he had the clause regarding Gemellus's inheritance annulled by declaring Tiberius insane, even though he let all other provisions in the will stand. Presumably, Tiberius was a man of very selective mental illness. Nevertheless, in March of 37 A.D., Caligula accepted the Senate's offering of the title of *Princeps*, and the new emperor rode into Rome to universal acclamation.

**Chapter 2: Descent into Madness**

"He who was born in the camp and reared 'mid the arms of his country,
Gave at the outset a sign that he was fated to rule."

The first months of Caligula's rule passed in a state akin to newly-wedded bliss. Rarely, if ever, had a ruler been the subject of such complete adoration upon his accession to the throne. Germanicus had been the darling of the Roman people, the dashing general who had won back the honor of Rome and avenged the dead of the Teutoburg Forest, and since his son had committed no public misdeeds, the Romans hoped Caligula would follow in his famous father's footsteps.

Furthermore, Tiberius, despite having been one of the most successful Emperors in terms of Roman expansion in the entire history of the Empire, had never been popular with the people, who felt he was too gloomy and too remote. His decision to choose self-exile in Capri and leave the day-to-day government to vastly unpopular figures like Sejanus had further turned the citizenry against him. Any alternative to Tiberius was bound to be a welcome one at first.

The Romans would be permanently scarred by 41 A.D., but Caligula initially proved to be an enlightened if somewhat populist monarch. One thing that stands out about Caligula's early reign is that he actually tried to court public favor. Suetonius recounted one of the young emperor's most famous acts:

"Gaius himself tried to rouse men's devotion by courting popularity in every way. After eulogising Tiberius with many tears before the assembled people and giving him a magnificent funeral, he at once posted off to Pandateria and the Pontian islands, to remove the ashes of his mother and brother to Rome; and in stormy weather, too, to make his filial piety the more conspicuous. He approached them with reverence and placed them in the urn with his own hands. With no less theatrical effect he brought them to Ostia in a bireme with a banner set in the stern, and from there up the Tiber to Rome, where he had them carried to the Mausoleum on two biers by the most distinguished men of the order of knights, in the middle of the day, when the streets were crowded. He appointed funeral sacrifices, too, to be offered each year with due ceremony, as well as games in the Circus in honour of his mother, providing a carriage to carry her image in the procession. But in memory of his father he gave to the month of September the name of Germanicus. After this, by a decree of the senate, he heaped upon his grandmother Antonia whatever honours Livia Augusta had ever enjoyed; took his uncle Claudius, who up to that time had been a Roman knight, as his colleague in the consulship; adopted his brother Tiberius on the day that he assumed the gown of manhood, and gave him the title of Chief of the Youth. He caused the names of his sisters to be included in all oaths: 'And I will not hold myself and my children dearer than I do Gaius and his sisters'; as well as in the propositions of the consuls: 'Favor and good fortune attend Gaius Caesar and his sisters.'"

**Eustache Le Sueur's 1647 painting, *Caligula Depositing the Ashes of his Mother and Brother in the Tomb of his Ancestors.***

Knowing that the army was his most powerful support base thanks to the love they had for Germanicus, one of Caligula's first moves was to grant substantial cash bonuses and shorten the terms of enlistment for much of the army. This included the Praetorian Guard, which was led by Macro and represented a large and menacing power looming behind the throne. He then ordered several of Tiberius's most unpopular edicts repealed, and he implemented a general pardon on all suspected acts of treason supposedly committed in the final years of Tiberius's reign. Naturally, this brought him no shortage of political support, because many prominent people had fallen foul of Tiberius's paranoia, and they were now able to return and reclaim their estates. Although it was too late to recall his mother and brothers from exile, Caligula made sure their remains were well-cared for. He had the decree by Tiberius which had publicly shamed Agrippina the Elder burned in public, and his ceremonial bearing of his family's remains to the mausoleum of Augustus made him seem like a model son.

Caligula also took care to ensure that the common people continued to support him. During the public acclamations that marked the first year of his rule, almost 200,000 animals were sacrificed to the gods and monumental gladiatorial games were staged free of charge for the benefit of the lower classes. Perhaps most ironically, Suetonius noted that Caligula "banished from the city the sexual perverts called spintriae", which earned him more public support.

Despite the difficulties of his teenage years, it appeared as though Caligula would be an effective, benevolent ruler. However, everything changed at some point near the end of 37 A.D., just months into Caligula's reign. The man who had first taken the throne was essentially never heard from again. As Suetonius aptly put it, "So much for Caligula as emperor; we must now tell of his career as a monster."

History is still unclear as to what set Caligula down his more notorious path. Suetonius doesn't even speculate as to the cause, but Philo of Alexandria wrote that Caligula was struck by a near-fatal illness, a mysterious disease which ancient sources did not describe in terms of symptoms. That has made it exceedingly difficult for contemporary scholars to come up with an accurate diagnosis with any certainty. However, it is likely that the illness, whatever it was, probably caused a severe fever. That fever might have led to Caligula developing a psychosis, but this is just one of dozens of possible diagnoses. It is also possible (though rather unlikely) that Caligula was never went mad at all, and that his subsequent actions were the product of a sane mind. Perhaps he may also have believed that his illness was an attempt to poison him, engendering a deep and abiding paranoia.

Whatever the cause, Caligula immediately started acting like a changed man near the end of 37 A.D. Shortly after the illness had almost killed him, Caligula ordered the arrest of his co-inheritor, Tiberius Gemellus. The charges brought against Gemellus were treason, so it is possible that Caligula felt that his recent disease had been an attempt by a disappointed Gemellus to remove him and thus claim what he rather rightly felt was his own inheritance. That action wouldn't have made Caligula seem crazy to the Romans, since it was politically rational to eliminate a rival. Caligula then ordered Gemellius to be quietly killed before his public trial, possibly to avoid a scandal. This action did little to endear him to his grandmother Antonia, who was also Gemellius's grandmother. She refused to speak or have anything to do with Caligula from then on, but shortly thereafter she also died mysteriously, allegedly of a broken heart. It appears far more likely, however, that Caligula had her murdered. If so, it was an act that couldn't have been justified, and it was made worse by the fact Antonia had cared for the young Caligula when he was alone and bereft of his mother and brothers.

Of all the things Caligula has become notorious for, incest is probably the best known. Caligula apparently took Julia Drusilla, his favorite sister, as his lover during this period. Although there is a possibility that the accusations of incest were merely malicious hearsay, there are several reasons to suppose that they were engaged in an amorous relationship, chief among them Caligula's dining habits. It was customary for an unmarried patrician to give the place of honor at his side during a banquet to his sister, and if he had multiple sisters, he would honor each of them in turn. However, in a grave breach of etiquette, Caligula insisted that only Julia Drusilla be granted this privilege, something which struck most observers as extremely bizarre, particularly because Caligula was notionally married to Lollia Paulina.

**Bust of Drusilla**

Making matters worse, even though Caligula seemed perfectly content to slight his wife in favor of his sister Drusilla, ancient writers claim that his other sister, Julia Livilla, was also involved in incestuous relationships with Caligula. As he descended into ever greater excesses, it was said that he even began ordering his sisters to engage in sexual relationships with his slaves.

It has been suggested that Agrippina the Younger, though married at this time, was also involved in Caligula's orgies. While all of these stories of incest have been taken at face value for thousands of years, the more lurid tales might possibly have been a malicious form of slander. But even if that was the case, it's apparent that Caligula had an unusual and apparently unhealthy relationship with his sisters, lavishing them with honours and favours far beyond what would be considered normal in Rome.

**Bust of Agrippina the Younger, who later became the mother of Nero.**

Caligula began to behave increasingly erratically. One of the first examples historians point to as evidence of his insanity was that he began to claim divinity. He apparently resented not being Augustus's direct descendant, so he began publicly claiming that Augustus had actually had an incestuous relationship with his own daughter, thus tightening the genealogical link between Caligula and the revered emperor. On top of that, Caligula went to extreme measures to let people know he was a god, according to Suetonius:

"But on being reminded that he had risen above the elevation both of princes and kings, he began from that time on to lay claim to divine majesty; for after giving orders that such statues of the gods as were especially famous for their sanctity or their artistic merit, including that of Jupiter of Olympia, should be brought from Greece, in order to remove their heads and put his own in their place, he built out a part of the Palace as far as the Forum, and making the temple of Castor and Pollux its vestibule, he often took his place between the divine brethren, and exhibited himself there to be worshipped by those who presented themselves; and some hailed him as Jupiter."

As if that wasn't enough, Caligula reportedly held conversations with the statues of the gods, sometimes yelling at them indignantly over some perceived slights. That was just one example of the way in which Caligula became extremely moody; he became prone to bouts of manic happiness and fits of rage that left even the members of his inner circle unsure whether they would live to see another day. Ultimately, the only person other than his sisters to survive Caligula's purges was his uncle Claudius. Though he would go on to become a successful emperor in his own right, Claudius was considered by Caligula and most of the Roman public as weak and feeble-minded. The young emperor probably kept Claudius around because he considered his uncle too pathetic to ever be much of a threat and because it amused him to mock his stuttering uncle's antics. Caligula was probably correct in judging Claudius to be no threat, but he treated his uncle more like a court jester than family member.

Caligula continued his hedonistic lifestyle in 38 A.D., squandering vast sums of money on profligate parties and orgies, but that year he suffered another personal tragedy when Drusilla, his favorite sister, died suddenly. A fever, one of the many sicknesses that periodically ran rampant through the overcrowded buildings of Rome, struck her down within a few days of the onset of the illness. Caligula was completely devastated. He had spent every hour by her side as she lingered, and after she died he shut himself away for days with her corpse, refusing anyone who attempted to take her away for burial.

Eventually, a delegation of Caligula's closest friends convinced him to allow Drusilla's body to be taken away so that it could be given the proper funerary honors before burial, but his loss seems to have aggravated his pre-existing psychosis. The emperor grew out his hair and beard and wore mourning dress like a widower would, and before having her interred he ordered the Senate to pass a motion deifying her as *Diva Drusilla* (Goddess Drusilla). He also ordered that she should be represented thereafter as Venus, goddess of love and beauty.

In the wake of Drusilla's death, Caligula was seemingly desperate for a distraction, and he got back into politics as a means of taking his mind off his grief. In 38 A.D., he published an edited version of the Imperial accounts, which Augustus had started but Tiberius kept secret. He also instituted a form of state-mandated insurance for Roman citizens who had lost wealth or property in the many fires that consistently flared up within the city. Caligula was also known for throwing expansive public spectacles, showering the people with gifts, free feasts, and trinkets, but at the same time he forbade public celebrations of Augustus's seminal victory over Antony at the Battle of Actium. In another populist move, he also reintroduced the practice of democratic election for government officials, one which had been gone since the rise to power of Caesar. He also expanded the Senate, as well as the *equites* (knights), to much grumbling and horror from the entrenched Roman aristocracy, who viewed such measures as mere philandering with no value and plenty of potential for damage.

After all these moves, not to mention Caligula's turn for the worse, the honeymoon was over. Caligula had started making more enemies than he could safely afford to have.

### Chapter 3: More Troubles

38 A.D. had been a miserable year from the beginning for Caligula, but it only continued to get worse. Before winter arrived, he ordered the summary execution of the Praetorian Prefect Macro, allegedly for plotting against him. This seemed to have been based on nothing other than paranoia, since Macro had been instrumental in placing Caligula upon the throne in the first place barely a year before. Macro wasn't the only victim of Caligula's paranoia; the emperor now saw plots coming from all angles. Suetonius wrote, "It would be trivial and pointless to add to this an account of his treatment of his relatives and friends, Ptolemy, son of king Juba, his cousin (for he was the grandson of Mark Antony by Antony's daughter Selene), and in particular Macro himself and even Ennia, who helped him to the throne; all these were rewarded for their kinship and their faithful services by a bloody death."

As it turned out, members of his own family may very well have begun plotting to murder him in 38 A.D., and the main architect of the plot was apparently Agrippina the Younger, a young woman whose machinations would have put many of the Borgias to shame. At the time, Agrippina was married to Gnaeus Domitius Ahenobarbus, and the year before she had given birth to Nero, a boy who would grow up to be almost as bad as his uncle. Gnaeus himself was a violent brute, and by all accounts Agrippina was no better. Despite her marriage, she seems to have had no compunction engaging in incestuous sexual activities with Caligula, and even if the ancient accounts of that incestuous relationship are dismissed as fabrication, it is almost certain that she did have a liaison with Marcus Aemilius Lepidus, Drusilla's recently widowed husband. It appears as though Livilla also took part in this affair, and that together the three of them conspired to murder Caligula and seize the throne for Lepidus. Incriminating letters indicating all this were produced by Caligula during their trial. At the same time, Livilla and Agrippina were already in a position of power and privilege far above any other woman in the empire, so it's unclear what they hoped to obtain from this conspiracy. Perhaps they had been forced into incest by Caligula against their will, or perhaps they figured that one of his uncontrollable fits of madness might lead to their deaths.

Either way, the conspiracy was a failure. They were betrayed or discovered (it is unclear which) and given a very public trial by Caligula, who was apparently unaware of any embarrassment the Imperial majesty might accrue by revealing that the Emperor's sisters were adulteresses who had conspired to murder him. The verdict was a simple formality. Lepidus was summarily executed, while Livilla and Agrippina were exiled to the Pontine Islands, but not before Caligula had sold virtually every garment and stick of furniture they possessed, condemning them to poverty.

Caligula must have been struck hard by such a betrayal by his closest and most privileged family members. Once again, he threw himself into affairs of state as a distraction, but even these proved painful. The Eastern provinces, particularly Egypt, were especially troublesome to him, especially since he felt they were being governed by incompetent leaders. He had several important imperial officials in the East executed. Caligula also failed to understand the fundamental religious differences that existed in the East, particularly the monotheistic traditions in Palestine. His response to turmoil among the Jews was to order the erection of statues of himself within their temples, ostensibly to promote loyalty. In the end, unrest in the Middle East would haunt Caligula until his dying day.

Caligula also focussed on affairs closer to home. In order to meet the ever-increasing demand for a reliable supply of grain, he had the harbor at Rhegium enlarged, and he began construction on two colossal and technologically superb aqueducts: the *Anio Novus* and the *Aqua Claudia*. Caligula also had a vast racetrack constructed, as well as the beginnings of an amphitheatre. The centerpiece of the racetrack was a colossal obelisk brought from Alexandria in a single piece at outrageous expense within the bowels of a specially constructed cargo ship. The obelisk still stands today at the center of St. Peter's Square in Rome.

Of course, Caligula also spent vast sums for his own personal pleasure. He significantly enlarged the Imperial quarters on the Palatine Hill, built several temples in honor of Augustus, and began extensive renovation works in several major Italian cities. He even had grand plans to build a mountain city in one of the high passes of the Alps, and the digging of a canal through the Isthmus of Corinth to increase shipping from the East. Caligula would run out of time to bring these plans to fruition.

Caligula's public works were extremely expensive, but they paled in comparison to the money he had squandered with his shameless pandering to the people and as a result of his own debauched lifestyle. It is estimated that Tiberius, over the course of his reign, had amassed almost three billion sestertii in the imperial coffers through the judicious administration of the wealth bestowed upon him by Augustus and careful husbanding of the Empire's resources. By the end of the first year of Caligula's reign, he had succeeded in squandering it all. Rome was bankrupt, so Caligula turned to every tyrant's last resort: the false accusation and execution of prominent patricians in order to seize their estates and wealth. A series of purges commenced, and scores of wealthy Roman aristocrats who had never dreamed of betrayal were suddenly accused of conspiring against the Emperor and put to death.

Even that was not enough. Caligula also began levying taxes on virtually everything he could think of, from marriage certificates to the earnings of prostitutes. Caligula retroactively altered Tiberius's will so he could claim that items granted to others were actually meant for him, and he seized others' assets with no qualms. Despite the dire financial straits he had placed the empire in, Caligula continued to hold lavish gladiatorial spectacles, but to make money he began auctioning the lives of the combatants off to the highest bidder.

Finally, in a move akin to political suicide, Caligula alienated the army almost entirely by insisting that any personal spoils taken by soldiers in the course of recent campaigns, particularly in Germania, be handed over as properly belonging to the Emperor. When even this did not suffice, Caligula extorted private citizens and borrowed from them at absurdly low interest rates, leaving the citizens well aware that the debt would never be repaid.

Rome was facing a calamity, and to top it off, a famine broke out in the city in the middle of 39 A.D. Thousands faced starvation, and for the first time, the people began turning against Caligula. Rumors of his lavish parties began to spread among the populace, many of whom were famished or watching loved ones grow steadily weaker. Caligula had managed to remain popular among the public due to the gifts he showered upon them since taking power, and his pro-democratic and populist stances had cemented that support, but the famine risked jeopardizing his standing among them.

In one of the most famous examples of having a tin ear, Caligula decided the proper response was not to attempt to solve the famine by selling state assets and buying more grain but to instead commence spending on two colossal private projects, both of which served no purpose other to gratify his ego.

The first project was the construction of two pleasure barges on Lake Nemi. While this enterprise would be par for the course for any emperor, the size of the boats was literally unprecedented in the ancient world. It is still unclear what the proportions of the lesser barge were, but the main vessel was nearly 350 feet long and 65 feet wide. It likely weighed about 8,000 tons and was crewed by nearly 1,000 sailors. To put this into perspective, today's largest privately owned yacht, Roman Abramovic's *Eclipse*, is only slightly longer than Caligula's pleasure ship.

Caligula's barge also boasted luxuries like marble floors and working plumbing, making it more similar to a modern cruise ship than an ancient galley. The boat used advanced water pumps and anchors, as well as the first evidence of the Romans' use of ball bearings, which Caligula apparently used to create a platform for a rotating statue. The technology aboard the Lake Nemi ships would not be widely used until the 19th century.

The ships at Nemi were perfect symbols for the excesses of Caligula, so after Caligula was assassinated, the ships were intentionally scuttled. Unfortunately, that was not the last time the ships met an untimely fate. Fishermen on the lake were aware of the boats' existence at the bottom for centuries, and Benito Mussolini ordered the lake partially drained to uncover the two ships. But in May 1944, during World War II, the Allies were pushing the Nazis north through Italy and a battle was waged in the area. On the night of May 31, the ships were almost completely destroyed in a fire. Both sides blamed the other.

**A picture of the hull of one of Caligula's ships on Lake Nemi**

The ships on Lake Nemi continue to generate interest, but they paled in comparison to Caligula's other costly project, which not only did nothing to solve the famine but in all likelihood actively contributed to it. Instead of using boats that were sorely needed to transport grain from Egypt, Caligula instead decided to build a bridge of boats about a mile long from Baiae to Puteoli in the gulf of Naples. Apparently, the bridge was built out of a desire to emulate what was the crowning act of *hubris* by one of antiquity's most reviled figures, the Persian emperor Xerxes. According to legend, Xerxes had famously built a bridge of boats across the Hellespont to transport his million-man army against the Greeks before the Spartans' famous stand at Thermopylae and the Greek victory at Plataea. Detailed accounts of the bridge's construction would have been available to Caligula and his court through the records left by Greek historians, but modern historians believe Xerxes's bridge never actually existed at all and was in reality either a failed attempt or a massive ferrying operation. Nevertheless, Caligula was determined to replicate it. There is also a legend, although it might well be apocryphal, that

Caligula had been told when he was just a young boy that it was as likely for him to ride across the bay of Naples as it would be for him to become Emperor, so Caligula was determined to physically ride across the bay.

Regardless of the rationale, the bridge was a truly massive undertaking, one that involved thousands of workers and took weeks if not months to complete. Once it was finished, the bridge stretched for almost a mile, and since the average cargo ship at the time probably had a width of around 30-45 feet, this would mean that at least 100 vessels and probably many more were used. These would have been anchored with giant pilings at both ends, but it is easy to underestimate the logistics of simply maneuvering the ships into place. Even with today's engines, it would still be a complex operation, but to complete it through the power of oars and sails alone is unbelievable. The project also would've required miles of ropes and cables possibly made out of extremely costly Nile papyrus, likely the only material strong enough to withstand the strains involved, just to keep the bridge together against the forces of winds, waves, and tide.

Once the bridge was completed, even more weight was added to the whole top-heavy structure by adding a wood-and-dirt roadway across the top of the anchored pontoons. Caligula even had rest stations built along the path so that he and his cortege could stop and refresh themselves. Once the bridge was completed, Caligula donned a breastplate allegedly belonging to Alexander the Great and then rode back and forth across it three times in grand style, followed by a vast retinue. While Xerxes had reportedly built the bridge to allow his army to cross the Hellespont and thus advance into Greece itself as part of a grand military campaign, the bridge Caligula constructed was completely useless. Travelling from Baiae to Puteoli by road would only require a further mile's worth of travel. Since it served no purpose, the bridge of boats was not properly maintained, and it quickly fell into disrepair, leaving its flotsam to choke up the bay.

### Chapter 4: A Fitting End

As Caligula's antics continued unabated, the Senate was understandably outraged and disgusted. Caligula also quickly discovered that by widening the Senatorial order, he had actually opened up the ranks of the Senate to even more people ready to hold a grudge against him, instead of winning him more support in that body. Even the men Caligula had pardoned after Tiberius had accused them of treachery could no longer be trusted. In a fit of spite, Caligula went over the tribunal records of the senators that had run afoul of Tiberius, and despite the fact he had pardoned so many of them just a few years earlier, he now convened new trials against senators. A series of purges ensued, during which the standing consul was forced to resign and dozens of Senators were put to death. Caligula continued to see conspiracies everywhere, and that view was possibly reasonable at this point given his behaviour. He had a number of prominent figures, including provincial governors, executed.

Of course, when Caligula acted violently to quash supposed conspiracies, it only induced more people to actually conspire against him. As if that wasn't enough, the Roman elite had to put up with watching Caligula dress up as Jupiter and other gods, something which deeply offended his more religious subjects.

Mired in a fog of suspicion and uncertainty, Caligula decided that the best way to distract the people and the Senate from the ever-pressing woes at home was to launch an aggressive military campaign of expansion. Naturally, he went about it in his own unusual way. The first territory Caligula annexed to the Roman Empire was Mauretania, a client kingdom of Rome ruled by the vassal monarch Ptolemy. For some reason, Caligula felt threatened by the eastern king, so he invited him to Rome under the pretense of staging a friendly banquet, only to have him arrested and executed. Without a king, and with Roman garrisons already massed along the border or in the country itself, Mauretania capitulated without a struggle and was later divided, in response to an internal uprising, into two provinces: Mauretania Caesarensis and Mauretania Tingitana. However, a bloodless "conquest" won by such deceit would not placate the Roman people, so Caligula planned a grand campaign to conquer Britannia, which quickly degenerated into a farce. Some modern historians have attempted to take a more generous outlook towards this venture, suggesting that the march to the English Channel was just a training mission, but the reality appears to have been simply a dismal failure.

After bombastic proclamations, Caligula dispatched a significant force into Gaul, from where they marched to the sea with the intention of crossing the channel and invading Britannia. Once there, it is said that the soldiers were enjoined to challenge Neptune himself, daring him to sink the invasion fleet just like Xerxes had the Hellespont whipped for defying his attempt to build a bridge of boats across the straits. But for reasons that remain unknown, due to a lack of records, the invasion of Britannia was never carried out. Back in Rome, a farcical and much-derided triumph was staged for Caligula's benefit, with the legionaries displaying shells and stones they had collected from the French coast as "spoils of war". Columns of chained "prisoners", who rather than being Britons were either Gaulish or Germanic slaves, were dressed up in what the Romans imagined to be traditional Britannic clothing. Needless to say, neither venture brought Caligula the glory and public acclamation he was hoping for.

By the end of 40 A.D., things were coming to a head. The people were tired of Caligula's empty promises and constant selfish spending, and money for public spectacles had long since dried out. The Senate and the equestrian orders were outraged by the constant witch hunts against alleged traitors, and even Caligula's old allies, the Praetorian Guard, were only lukewarm in their support. Caligula even distrusted his new wife, Caesonia, even though she had given him a daughter, named Julia Drusilla after his beloved sister. By the end, the only people he trusted were his personal bodyguards, recruited among the fierce Germans across the Rhine.

However, such a situation could not last. The end came on January 24th, 41 A.D. Caligula had been overseeing the rehearsals for a spectacle in honor of the memory of Augustus, when, on his way out of the theater, he entered a *cryptoporticus*, an underground tunnel. It was at this moment, when he was in a vulnerable position ripe for ambush, that the long-feared conspirators struck. They were led by Cassius Chaerea, a Praetorian Guardsman with a longstanding grudge against Caligula. For years, Caligula had cruelly mocked Chaerea, making snide comments about his ostensibly feminine voice by calling him "Venus". Caligula also occasionally called him "Priapus", a crude Roman fertility god whose chief attribute was a large erection. Chaerea and his conspirators are said to have acted alone, but it appears likely that large numbers of Senators were aware of the conspiracy and simply chose to do nothing.

Once Caligula was in the *cryptoporticus*, Chaerea and his co-conspirators, armed with knives, set upon him in a savage attack. In a scene eerily reminiscent of Julius Caesar's death, Caligula was stabbed thirty times, presumably dying of blood-loss and associated trauma. Chaerea and some of the other conspirators managed to escape, but others were still in the tunnel along with a number of innocent and shocked bystanders (including several Senators) when the Germanic bodyguard arrived on the scene. In a fit of rage, the fierce warriors attacked anyone who was still present indiscriminately, hewing down a large number of unfortunate civilians who had no part in the attack.

Meanwhile, Chaerea and the other survivors of the attack made their way into the palace, where word of the Emperor's death had not yet spread. In order to ensure there would be no successor from Caligula's own bloodline, they murdered his wife Caesonia and killed the infant Julia Drusilla by smashing her head against a wall.

As news of Caligula's death spread, tension in the city grew, and many people, including Chaerea himself, clamored for a return to power of the Senate. Although the Senators would have wanted nothing more than to regain the power they had held before the Republic fell, and which they had all but exercised when Tiberius retired to Capri, the Roman army stubbornly stayed loyal to the Imperial office. They forced the Senate to stand by as Claudius, the most eligible by blood and least likely by logic, was handpicked to become Emperor. His rule would not be overly long, and it would be followed shortly thereafter by Caligula's nephew Nero, a man whose excesses sometimes made Caligula seem tame.

### Chapter 5: Caligula's Legacy

To this day, Caligula survives in popular imagination as a vile human being. He is one of the main villains in Rupert Graves's classic *I, Claudius*, and he was also the protagonist of a notorious 1979 cult film, *Caligula*, penned by Gore Vidal, which is still banned in many countries due to its high emphasis upon graphic sex and violence. By all accounts, the film was not wide of the mark in terms of Caligula's behavior.

For nearly 2,000 years, Caligula has been universally viewed as a despotic and despicable tyrant, a man who murdered at a whim and who engaged in every vice available to someone in a position of absolute power. Caligula is the man who had incestuous relationships with virtually every female member of his family, threatened to make his horse a Senator (and did make the horse a priest), and built a bridge of boats connecting two ends of a bay for no other reason than that he wished to ride across water. While there are apparently at least kernels of truth to all these legends, it is worth remembering that, no matter how absurd his excesses, Caligula was a real man who did not behave the way he did in an effort to be a cartoonish caricature of an evil villain. It seems unlikely that Caligula's psychosis was a consequence of a particularly unhealthy family upbringing, a common cause of mental illness. His father was a well-respected man who doted on his little boy, and his mother was a noblewoman who did not display any abusive behaviour. Instead, it seems that Caligula fell prey to a debilitating disease that literally made him go crazy. While Caligula's life and exploits have become the stuff of legends, and his worst excesses are portrayed colorfully and at times almost humorously, the fact that a mental illness seemed to turn a decent ruler into history's biggest madman also makes Caligula a somewhat tragic figure.

Caligula, like most tyrants of his ilk, died prematurely and violently. Perhaps it's surprising that he lasted so long in the first place. Unlike other Roman emperors who were personally despicable and loathed by those aware of their private activities, Caligula managed to alienate the public as well. Moreover, while Caligula was almost certainly mentally ill, the behavior of his sisters was also remarkably sociopathic. It is unclear to what extent they were willing participants in his excesses, or whether they were simply afraid for their lives, but Agrippina the Younger cannot claim fear as the motivation for her acts. Even after Caligula's death, she continued to engage in all kinds of sadistic and immoral acts, including poisoning her husband Claudius to bring her son Nero to power.

Ultimately, Caligula remains a nebulous figure. The available sources on his reign are incomplete or address much of what he did only tangentially. Suetonius's description of Caligula's life and reign, which is included below as an appendix, concentrates almost entirely on describing Caligula's bizarre activities. There were far more comprehensive histories, possibly including Tacitus's *Annals*, but they did not survive antiquity. Some of the ancient works were written while Caligula was still alive or in the immediate wake of his short reign, so historians are wary about trusting them entirely. Nevertheless, everyone agrees that Caligula suffered from some form of psychosis, either caused or exacerbated by his illness in 37 A.D. and then exacerbated by the death of Julia Drusilla the following year. And even if he was certifiably insane, his repugnant behaviour and lavish excesses cannot be justified or excused under any circumstances. Caligula bankrupted the Imperial coffers, committed all sorts of state violence against innocent Romans, engaged in unspeakable sexual perversions, and caused an undue amount of grief. Even his construction projects come across as being maliciously useless.

Caligula's legend has grown over the centuries, but the facts behind the legend, which are just as outlandish as the stories they inspired, appear to be firmly grounded in truth. Unlike Nero, whose enmity towards Christians was a significant influence on religious-based histories of him, or Commodus, who had the misfortune to follow in the footsteps of one of the greatest minds in Western philosophy (Marcus Aurelius), it does not appear as though the Romans held any bias against Caligula. Seneca, one of the very few surviving contemporary sources of the notorious emperor, had no cause to love him since he was nearly put to death for his alleged involvement in a conspiracy, but other writers like Suetonius cast him as evil and lunacy incarnate. Caligula succeeded the vastly (albeit rather unfairly) disliked Tiberius, he was from the same family as the beloved Julius Caesar and Augustus, the common people did not suffer unduly because of his policies, and he did not suffer any grievous military reverses. Therefore, it is reasonable to assume that everything currently known about Caligula, including even the most lurid stories, is at the very least based somewhat on fact.

All things considered, Caligula earned his place within the pantheon of history's most villainous rulers.

## Suetonius's Life of Caligula

1   1. Germanicus, father of Gaius Caesar, son of Drusus and the younger Antonia, after being adopted by his paternal uncle Tiberius, held the quaestorship five years before the legal age and passed directly to the consulship. When the death of Augustus was announced, he was sent to the army in Germany, where it is hard to say whether his filial piety or his courage was more conspicuous; for although all the legions obstinately refused to accept Tiberius as emperor, and offered him the rule of the state, he held them to their allegiance. And later he won a victory over the enemy and celebrated a triumph. 2 Then chosen consul for a second time, before he entered on his term he was hurried off to restore order in the Orient, and after vanquishing the king of Armenia and reducing Cappadocia to the form of a province, died of a lingering illness at Antioch, in the thirty-fourth year of his age. There was some suspicion that he was poisoned; for besides the dark spots which appeared all over his body and the froth which flowed from his mouth, after he had been reduced to ashes his heart was found entire among his bones; and it is supposed to be a characteristic of that organ that when steeped in poison it cannot be destroyed by fire.

2   1 Now the belief was that he met his death through the wiles of Tiberius, aided and abetted by Gnaeus Piso. This man had been made governor of Syria at about that time, and realising that he must give offence either to the father or the son, as if there were no alternative, he never ceased to show the bitterest enmity towards Germanicus in word and deed, even after the latter fell ill. In consequence Piso narrowly escaped being torn to pieces by the people on his return to Rome, and was condemned to death by the senate.

3  1 It is the general opinion that Germanicus possessed all the highest qualities of body and mind, to a degree never equalled by anyone; a handsome person, a unequalled valour, surpassing ability in the oratory and learning of Greece and Rome, unexampled kindliness, and a remarkable desire and capacity for winning men's regard and inspiring their affection. His legs were too slender for the rest of his figure, but he gradually brought them to proper proportions by constant horseback riding after meals. 2 He often slew a foeman in hand-to-hand combat. He pleaded causes even after receiving the triumphal regalia; and among other fruits of his studies he left some Greek comedies. Unassuming at home and abroad, he always entered the free and federate towns without lictors. Wherever he came upon the tombs of distinguished men, he always offered sacrifice to their shades. Planning to bury in one mound the old and scattered relics of those who fell in the overthrow of Varus, he was the first to attempt to collect and assemble them with his own hand. 3 Even towards his detractors, whosoever they were and whatever their motives, he was so mild and lenient, that when Piso was annulling his decrees and maltreating his dependents, he could not make up his mind to break with him, until he found himself assailed also by potions and spells. Even then he went no further than formally to renounce Piso's friendship in the old-time fashion, and to bid his household avenge him, in case anything should befall him.


4  1 He reaped plentiful fruit from these virtues, for he was so respected and beloved by his kindred that Augustus (to say nothing of the rest of his relatives) after hesitating for a long time whether to appoint him his successor, had him adopted by Tiberius. He was so popular with the masses, that, according to many writers, whenever he came to any place or left one, he was sometimes in danger of his life from the crowds that met him or saw him off; in fact, when he returned from Germany after quelling the outbreak, all the cohorts of the praetorian guard went forth to meet him, although orders had been given that only two should go, and the whole populace, regardless of age, sex, or rank, poured out of Rome as far as the twentieth milestone.


5  1 Yet far greater and stronger tokens of regard were shown at the time of his death and immediately afterwards. On the day when he passed away the temples were stoned and the altars of the gods thrown down, while some flung their household gods into the street and cast out their newly born children. Even barbarian peoples, so they say, who were engaged in war with us or with one another, unanimously consented to a truce, as if all in common had suffered a domestic tragedy. It is said that some princes put off their beards and had their wives' heads shaved, as a token of the deepest mourning; that even the king of kings suspended his exercise at hunting and the banquets with his grandees, which among the Parthians is a sign of public mourning.

6  1 At Rome when the community, in grief and consternation at the first report of his illness, was awaiting further news, and suddenly after nightfall a report at last spread abroad, on doubtful authority, that he had recovered, a general rush was made from every side to the Capitol with torches and victims, and the temple gates were all but torn off, that nothing might hinder them in their eagerness to pay their vows. Tiberius was roused from sleep by the cries of the rejoicing throng, who all united in singing:—

"Safe is Rome, safe too our country, for Germanicus is safe."

2 But when it was at last made known that he was no more, the public grief could be checked neither by any consolation nor edict, and it continued even during the festal days of the month of December.

The fame of the deceased and regret for his loss were increased by the horror of the times which followed, since all believed, and with good reason, that the cruelty of Tiberius, which soon burst forth, had been held in check through his respect and awe for Germanicus.

7    1 He had to wife Agrippina, daughter of Marcus Agrippa and Julia, who bore him nine children. Two of these were taken off when they were still in infancy, and one just as he was reaching the age of boyhood, a charming child, whose statue, in the guise of Cupid, Livia dedicated in the temple of the Capitoline Venus, while Augustus had another placed in his bed chamber and used to kiss it fondly whenever he entered the room. The other children survived their father, three girls, Agrippina, Drusilla, and Livilla, born in successive years, and three boys, Nero, Drusus, and Gaius Caesar. Nero and Drusus were adjudged public enemies by the senate on the accusation of Tiberius.

8    1 Gaius Caesar was born the day before the Kalends of September in the consulship of his father and Gaius Fonteius Capito. Conflicting testimony makes his birthplace uncertain. Gnaeus Lentulus Gaetulicus writes that he was born at Tibur, Plinius Secundus among the Treveri, in a village called Ambitarvium above the Confluence. Pliny adds as proof that altars are shown there, inscribed "For the Delivery of Agrippina." Verses which were in circulation soon after he became emperor indicate that he was begotten in the winter-quarters of the legions:

"He who was born in the camp and reared 'mid the arms of his country,

Gave at the outset a sign that he was fated to rule."

2 I myself find in the gazette that he first saw the light at Antium. Gaetulicus is shown to be wrong by Pliny, who says that he told a flattering lie, to add some lustre to the fame of a young and vainglorious prince from the city sacred to Hercules; and that he lied with the more assurance because Germanicus really did have a son born to him at Tibur, also called Gaius Caesar, of whose lovable disposition and untimely death I have already spoken. Pliny has erred in his chronology; 3 for the historians of Augustus agree that Germanicus was not sent to Germany until the close of his consulship, when Gaius was already born. Moreover, the inscription on the altar adds no strength to Pliny's view, for Agrippina twice gave birth to daughters in that region, and any childbirth, regardless of sex, is called puerperium, since the men of old called girls puerae, just as they called boys puelli. 4 Furthermore, we have a letter written by Augustus to his granddaughter Agrippina, a few months before he died, about the Gaius in question (for no other child of the name was still alive at that time), reading as follows: "Yesterday I arranged with Talarius and Asillius to bring your boy Gaius on the fifteenth day before the Kalends of June, if it be the will of the gods. I send with him besides one of my slaves who is a physician, and I have written Germanicus to keep him if he wishes. Farewell, my own Agrippina, and take care to come in good health to your Germanicus."

5 I think it is clear enough that Gaius could not have been born in a place to which he was first taken from Rome when he was nearly two years old. This letter also weakens our confidence in the verses, the more so because they are anonymous. We must then accept the only remaining testimony, that of the public record, particularly since Gaius loved Antium as if it were his native soil, always preferring it to all other places of retreat, and even thinking, it is said, of transferring there the seat and abode of the empire through weariness of Rome.

9  1 His surname Caligula he derived from a joke of the troops, because he was brought up in their midst in the dress of a common soldier. To what extent besides he won their love and devotion by being reared in fellowship with them is especially evident from the fact that when they threatened mutiny after the death of Augustus and were ready for any act of madness, the mere sight of Gaius unquestionably calmed them. For they did not become quiet until they saw that he was being spirited away because of the danger from their outbreak and taken for protection to the nearest town. Then at last they became contrite, and laying hold of the carriage and stopping it, begged to be spared the disgrace which was being put upon them.

10   1 He attended his father also on his expedition to Syria. On his return from there he first lived with his mother and after her banishment, with his great-grandmother Livia; and when Livia died, though he was not yet of age, he spoke her eulogy from the rostra. Then he fell to the care of his grandmother Antonia and in the nineteenth year of his age he was called to Capreae by Tiberius, on the same day assuming the gown of manhood and shaving his first beard, but without any such ceremony as had attended the coming of age of his brothers. 2 Although at Capreae every kind of wile was resorted to by those who tried to lure him or force him to utter complaints, he never gave them any satisfaction, ignoring the ruin of his kindred as if nothing at all had happened, passing over his own ill-treatment with an incredible pretence of indifference, and so obsequious towards his grandfather and his household, that it was well said of him that no one had ever been a better slave or a worse master.


11   Yet even at that time he could not control his natural cruelty and viciousness, but he was a most eager witness of the tortures and executions of those who suffered punishment, revelling at night in gluttony and adultery, disguised in a wig and a long robe, passionately devoted besides to the theatrical arts of dancing and singing, in which Tiberius very willingly indulged him, in the hope that through these his savage nature might be softened. This last was so clearly evident to the shrewd old man, that he used to say now and then that to allow Gaius to live would prove the ruin of himself and of all men, and that he was rearing a viper for the Roman people and a Phaethon for the world.


12   1 Not so very long afterward Gaius took to wife Junia Claudilla, daughter of Marcus Silanus, a man of noble rank. Then appointed augur in place of his brother Drusus, before he was invested with the office he was advanced to that of pontiff, with strong commendation of his dutiful conduct and general character; for since the court was deserted and deprived of its other supports, after Sejanus had been suspected of hostile designs and presently put out of the way, he was little by little encouraged to look forward to the succession. 2 To have a better chance of realising this, after losing Junia in childbirth, he seduced Ennia Naevia, wife of Macro, who at that time commanded the praetorian guard, even promising to marry her if he became emperor, and guaranteeing this promise by an oath and a written contract. Having through her wormed himself into Macro's favour, he poisoned Tiberius, as some think, and ordered that his ring be taken from him while he still breathed, and then suspecting that he was trying to hold fast to it, that a pillow be put over his face; or even strangled the old man with his own hand, immediately ordering the crucifixion of a freedman who cried out at the awful deed. 3 And this is likely enough; for some writers say that Caligula himself later admitted, not it is true that he had committed parricide, but that he had at least meditated it at one time; for they say that he constantly boasted, in speaking of his filial piety, that he had entered the bedchamber of the

sleeping Tiberius dagger in hand, to avenge the death of his mother and brothers; but that, seized with pity, he threw down the dagger and went out again; and that though Tiberius knew of this, he had never dared to make any inquiry or take any action.

13   1 By thus gaining the throne he fulfilled the highest hopes of the Roman people, or I may say of all mankind, since he was the prince most earnestly desired by the great part of the provincials and soldiers, many of whom had known him in his infancy, as well as by the whole body of the city populace, because of the memory of his father Germanicus and pity for a family that was all but extinct. Accordingly, when he set out from Misenum, though he was in mourning garb and escorting the body of Tiberius, yet his progress was marked by altars, victims, and blazing torches, and he was met by a dense and joyful throng, who called him besides other propitious names their "star," their "chick," their "babe," and their "nursling."

14   1 When he entered the city, full and absolute power was at once put into his hands by the unanimous consent of the senate and of the mob, which forced its way into the House, and no attention was paid to the wish of Tiberius, who in his will had named his other grandson, still a boy, joint heir with Caligula. So great was the public rejoicing, that within the next three months, or less than that, more than a hundred and sixty thousand victims are said to have been slain in sacrifice.

2 A few days after this, when he crossed to the islands near Campania, vows were put up for his safe return, while no one let slip even the slightest chance of giving testimony to his anxiety and regard for his safety. But when he fell ill, they all spent the whole night about the Palace; some even vowed to fight as gladiators, and others posted placards offering their lives, if the ailing prince were spared. 3 To this unbounded love of his citizens was added marked devotion from foreigners. Artabanus, for example, king of the Parthians, who was always outspoken in his hatred and contempt for Tiberius, voluntarily sought Caligula's friendship and came to a conference with the consular governor; then crossing the Euphrates, he paid homage to the Roman eagles and standards and to the statues of the Caesars.

15   1 Gaius himself tried to rouse men's devotion by courting popularity in every way. After eulogising Tiberius with many tears before the assembled people and giving him a magnificent funeral, he at once posted off to Pandateria and the Pontian islands, to remove the ashes of his mother and brother to Rome; and in stormy weather, too, to make his filial piety the more

conspicuous. He approached them with reverence and placed them in the urn with his own hands. With no less theatrical effect he brought them to Ostia in a bireme with a banner set in the stern, and from there up the Tiber to Rome, where he had them carried to the Mausoleum on two biers by the most distinguished men of the order of knights, in the middle of the day, when the streets were crowded. He appointed funeral sacrifices, too, to be offered each year with due ceremony, as well as games in the Circus in honour of his mother, providing a carriage to carry her image in the procession. 2 But in memory of his father he gave to the month of September the name of Germanicus. After this, by a decree of the senate, he heaped upon his grandmother Antonia whatever honours Livia Augusta had ever enjoyed; took his uncle Claudius, who up to that time had been a Roman knight, as his colleague in the consulship; adopted his brother Tiberius on the day that he assumed the gown of manhood, and gave him the title of Chief of the Youth. 3 He caused the names of his sisters to be included in all oaths: "And I will not hold myself and my children dearer than I do Gaius and his sisters"; as well as in the propositions of the consuls: "Favour and good fortune attend Gaius Caesar and his sisters."


4 With the same degree of popularity he recalled those who had been condemned to banishment; took no cognizance of any charges that remained untried from an earlier time; had all documents relating to the cases of his mother and brothers carried to the Forum and burned, to give no informer or witness occasion for further fear, having first loudly called the gods to witness that he had neither read nor touched any of them. He refused a note which was offered him regarding his own safety, maintaining that he had done nothing to make anyone hate him, and that he had no ears for informers.


16  1 He banished from the city the sexual perverts called spintriae, barely persuaded not to sink them in the sea. The writings of Titus Labienus, Cremutius Cordus, and Cassius Severus, which had been suppressed by decrees of the senate, he allowed to be hunted up, circulated, and read, saying that it was wholly to his interest that everything which happened be handed down to posterity. He published the accounts of the empire, which had regularly been made public by Augustus, a practice discontinued by Tiberius. 2 He allowed the magistrates unrestricted jurisdiction, without appeal to himself. He revised the lists of the Roman knights strictly and scrupulously, yet with due moderation, publicly taking their horses from those guilty of any wicked or scandalous act, but merely omitting to read the names of men convicted of lesser offences. To lighten the labour of the jurors, he added a fifth division to the previous four. He tried also to restore the suffrage to the people by reviving the custom of elections. 3 He at once paid faithfully and without dispute the legacies named in the will of Tiberius, though this had been set aside, as well as in that of Julia Augusta, which Tiberius had suppressed. He remitted the tax of a two-hundredth on auction sales in Italy; made good to many their losses from fires;

and whenever he restored kings to their thrones, he allowed them all the arrears of their taxes and their revenue for the meantime; for example, to Antiochus of Commagene, a hundred million sesterces that had accrued to the Treasury. 4 To make it known that he encouraged every kind of noble action, he gave eight hundred thousand sesterces to a freedwoman, because she had kept silence about the guilt of her patron, though subjected to the utmost torture. Because of these acts, besides other honours, a golden shield was voted him, which was to be borne every year to the Capitol on an appointed day by the colleges of priests, escorted by the senate, while boys and girls of noble birth sang the praises of his virtues in a choral ode. It was further decreed that the day on which he began to reign should be called the •Parilia, as a token that the city had been founded a second time.

17  1 He held four consulships, one from the Kalends of July for two months, a second from the Kalends of January for thirty days, a third up to the Ides of January, and the fourth until the seventh day before the Ides of the same month. Of all these only the last two were continuous. The third he assumed at Lugdunum without a colleague, not, as some think, through arrogance or disregard of precedent, but because at that distance from Rome he had been unable to get news of the death of the other consul just before the day of the Kalends. 2 He twice gave the people a largess of three hundred sesterces each, and twice a lavish banquet to the senate and the equestrian order, together with their wives and children. At the former of these he also distributed togas to the men, and to the women and children scarves of red and scarlet. Furthermore, to make a permanent addition to the public gaiety, he added a day to the Saturnalia, and called it Juvenalis.

18  1 He gave several gladiatorial shows, some in the amphitheatre of Taurus and some in the •Saepta, in which he introduced pairs of African and Campanian boxers, the pick of both regions. He did not always preside at the games in person, but sometimes assigned the honour to the magistrates or to friends. 2 He exhibited stage-plays continually, of various kinds and in many different places, sometimes even by night, lighting up the whole city. He also threw about gifts of various kinds, and gave each man a basket of victuals. During the feasting he sent his share to a Roman knight opposite him, who was eating with evident relish and appetite, while to a senator for the same reason he gave a commission naming him praetor out of the regular order. 3 He also gave many games in the Circus, lasting from early morning until evening, introducing between the races now a baiting of panthers and now the manoeuvres of the game called Troy; some, too, of special splendour, in which the Circus was strewn with red and green, while the charioteers were all men of senatorial rank. He also started some games off-hand, when a few people called for them from the neighbouring balconies, as he was inspecting the outfit of the Circus from the Gelotian house.

19   1 Besides this, he devised a novel and unheard of kind of pageant; for he bridged the gap between Baiae and the mole at Puteoli, a distance of about thirty-six hundred paces, by bringing together merchant ships from all sides and anchoring them in a double line, afterwards a mound of earth was heaped upon them and fashioned in the manner of the Appian Way. 2 Over this bridge he rode back and forth for two successive days, the first day on a caparisoned horse, himself resplendent in a crown of oak leaves, a buckler, a sword, and a cloak of cloth of gold; on the second, in the dress of a charioteer in a car drawn by a pair of famous horses, carrying before him a boy named Dareus, one of the hostages from Parthia, and attended by the entire praetorian guard and a company of his friends in Gallic chariots. 3 I know that many have supposed that Gaius devised this kind of bridge in rivalry of Xerxes, who excited no little admiration by bridging the much narrower Hellespont; others, that it was to inspire fear in Germany and Britain, on which he had designs, by the fame of some stupendous work. But when I was a boy, I used to hear my grandfather say that the reason for the work, as revealed by the emperor's confidential courtiers, was that Thrasyllus the astrologer had declared to Tiberius, when he was worried about his successor and inclined towards his natural grandson, that Gaius had no more chance of becoming emperor than of riding about over the gulf of Baiae with horses.

20   1 He also gave shows in foreign lands, Athenian games at Syracuse in Sicily, and miscellaneous games at Lugdunum in Gaul; at the latter place also a contest in Greek and Latin oratory, in which, they say, the losers gave prizes to the victors and were forced to compose eulogies upon them, while those who were least successful were ordered to erase their writings with a sponge or with their tongue, unless they elected rather to be beaten with rods or thrown into the neighbouring river.

21   1 He completed the public works which had been half finished under Tiberius, namely the temple of Augustus and the •theatre of Pompey. He likewise began an aqueduct in the region near Tibur and an amphitheatre beside the Saepta, the former finished by his successor Claudius, while the latter was abandoned. At Syracuse he repaired the city walls, which had fallen into ruin though lapse of time, and the temples of the gods. He had planned, besides, to rebuild the palace of Polycrates at Samos, to finish the temple of Didymaean Apollo at Ephesus, to found a city high up in the Alps, but, above all, to dig a canal through the Isthmus in Greece, and he had already sent a chief centurion to survey the work.

22   1 So much for Caligula as emperor; we must now tell of his career as a monster.

After he had assumed various surnames (for he was called "Pious," "Child of the Camp," "Father of the Armies," and "Greatest and Best of Caesars"), chancing to overhear some kings, who had come to Rome to pay their respects to him, disputing at dinner about the nobility of their descent, he cried:

"Let there be one Lord, one King."

And he came near assuming a crown at once and changing the semblance of a principate into the form of a monarchy. 2 But on being reminded that he had risen above the elevation both of princes and kings, he began from that time on to lay claim to divine majesty; for after giving orders that such statues of the gods as were especially famous for their sanctity or their artistic merit, including that of Jupiter of Olympia, should be brought from Greece, in order to remove their heads and put his own in their place, he built out a part of the Palace as far as the Forum, and making the temple of Castor and Pollux its vestibule, he often took his place between the divine brethren, and exhibited himself there to be worshipped by those who presented themselves; and some hailed him as Jupiter Latiaris. 3 He also set up a special temple to his own godhead, with priests and with victims of the choicest kind. In this temple was a life-sized statue of the emperor in gold, which was dressed each day in clothing such as he wore himself. The richest citizens used all their influence to secure the priesthoods of his cult and bid high for the honour. The victims were flamingoes, peacocks, black grouse, guinea-hens and pheasants, offered day by day each after its own kind. 4 At night he used constantly to invite the full and radiant moon to his embraces and his bed, while in the daytime he would talk confidentially with Jupiter Capitolinus, now whispering and then in turn his ear to the mouth of the god, now in louder and even angry language; for he was heard to make the threat: "Lift me up, or I'll lift thee." But finally won by entreaties, as he reported, and even invited to live with the god, he built a bridge over the temple to the Deified Augustus, and thus joined his Palace to the Capitol. Presently, to be nearer yet, he laid the foundations of a new house in the court of the Capitol.

23   1 He did not wish to be thought the grandson of Agrippa, or called so, because of the latter's humble origin; and he grew very angry if anyone in a speech or a song included Agrippa among the ancestors of the Caesars. He even boasted that his own mother was born in incest, which Augustus had committed with his daughter Julia; and not content with this slur on the memory of Augustus, he forbade the celebration of his victories at Actium and off Sicily by annual festivals, on the ground that they were disastrous and ruinous to the Roman people. 2 He often called his great-grandmother Livia Augusta "a Ulysses in petticoats," and he had the audacity to accuse her of low birth in a letter to the senate, alleging that her maternal grandfather

had been nothing but a decurion of Fundi; whereas it is proved by public records that Aufidius Lurco held high offices at Rome. When his grandmother Antonia asked for a private interview, he refused it except in the presence of the praefect Macro, and by such indignities and annoyances he caused her death; although some think that he also gave her poison. After she was dead, he paid her no honour, but viewed her burning pyre from his dining-room. 3 He had his brother Tiberius put to death without warning, suddenly sending a tribune of the soldiers to do the deed; besides driving his father-in-law Silanus to end his life by cutting his throat with a razor. His charge against the latter was that Silanus had not followed him when he put to sea in stormy weather, but had remained behind in the hope of taking possession of the city in case he should be lost in the storm; against Tiberius, that his breath smelled of an antidote, which he had taken to guard against being poisoned at his hand. Now as a matter of fact, Silanus was subject to sea-sickness and wished to avoid the discomforts of the voyage, while Tiberius had taken medicine for a chronic cough, which was growing worse. As for his uncle Claudius, he spared him merely as a laughing-stock.

24   1 He lived in habitual incest with all his sisters, and at a large banquet he placed each of them in turn below him, while his wife reclined above. Of these he is believed to have violated Drusilla when he was still a minor, and even to have been caught lying with her by his grandmother Antonia, at whose house they were brought up in company. Afterwards, when she was the wife of Lucius Cassius Longinus, an ex-consul, he took her from him and openly treated her as his lawful wife; and when ill, he made her heir to his property and the throne. 2 When she died, he appointed a season of public mourning, during which it was a capital offence to laugh, bathe, or dine in company with one's parents, wife, or children. He was so beside himself with grief that suddenly fleeing the city by night and traversing Campania, he went to Syracuse and hurriedly returned from there without cutting his hair or shaving his beard. And he never afterwards took oath about matters of the highest moment, even before the assembly of the people or in the presence of the soldiers, except by the godhead of Drusilla. 3 The rest of his sisters he did not love with so great affection, nor honour so highly, but often prostituted them to his favourites; so that he was the readier at the trial of Aemilius Lepidus to condemn them, as adulteresses and privy to the conspiracies against him; and he not only made public letters in the handwriting of all of them, procured by fraud and seduction, but also dedicated to Mars the Avenger, with an explanatory inscription, three swords designed to take his life.

25   1 It is not easy to decide whether he acted more basely in contracting his marriages, in annulling them, or as a husband. At the marriage of Livia Orestilla to Gaius Piso, he attended the ceremony himself, gave orders that the bride be taken to his own house, and within a few days divorced her; two years later he banished her, because of a suspicion that in the meantime she

had gone back to her former husband. Others write that being invited to the wedding banquet, he sent word to Piso, who reclined opposite to him: "Don't take liberties with my wife," and at once carried her off with him from the table, the next day issuing a proclamation that he had got himself a wife in the manner of Romulus and Augustus. 2 When the statement was made that the grandmother of Lollia Paulina, who was married to Gaius Memmius, an ex-consul commanding armies, had once been a remarkably beautiful woman, he suddenly called Lollia from the province, separated her from her husband, and married her; then in a short time had her put away, with the command never to have intercourse with anyone. 3 Though Caesonia was neither beautiful nor young, and was already mother of three daughters by another, besides being a woman of reckless extravagance and wantonness, he loved her not only more passionately but more faithfully, often exhibiting her to the soldiers riding by his side, decked with cloak, helmet and shield, and to his friends even in a state of nudity. He did not honour her with the title of wife until she had borne him a child, announcing on the selfsame day that he had married her and that he was the father of her babe. 4 This babe, whom he named Julia Drusilla, he carried to the temples of all the goddesses, finally placing her in the lap of Minerva and commending to her the child's nurture and training. And no evidence convinced him so positively that she was sprung from his own loins as her savage temper, which was even then so violent that she would try to scratch the faces and eyes of the little children who played with her.

26  1 It would be trivial and pointless to add to this an account of his treatment of his relatives and friends, Ptolemy, son of king Juba, his cousin (for he was the grandson of Mark Antony by Antony's daughter Selene), and in particular Macro himself and even Ennia, who helped him to the throne; all these were rewarded for their kinship and their faithful services by a bloody death.

2 He was no whit more respectful or mild towards the senate, allowing some who had held the highest offices to run in their togas for several miles beside his chariot and to wait on him at table, standing napkin in hand either at the head of his couch, or at his feet. Others he secretly put to death, yet continued to send for them as if they were alive, after a few days falsely asserting that they had committed suicide. 3 When the consuls forgot to make proclamation of his birthday, he deposed them, and left the state for three days without its highest magistrates. He flogged his quaestor, who was charged with conspiracy, stripping off the man's clothes and spreading them under the soldiers' feet, to give them a firm footing as they beat him.

4 He treated the other orders with like insolence and cruelty. Being disturbed by the noise made by those who came in the middle of the night to secure the free seats in the Circus, he drove them all out with cudgels; in the confusion more than twenty Roman knights were crushed

to death, with as many matrons and a countless number of others. At the plays in the theatre, sowing discord between the commons and the knights, he scattered the gift tickets ahead of time, to induce the rabble to take the seats reserved for the equestrian order. 5 At a gladiatorial show he would sometimes draw back the awnings when the sun was hottest and give orders that no one be allowed to leave; then removing the usual equipment, he would match worthless decrepit gladiators against mangy wild beasts, and have sham fights between householders who were of good repute, but conspicuous for some bodily infirmity. Sometimes too he would shut up the granaries and condemn the people to hunger.

27  1 The following are special instances of his innate brutality. When cattle to feed the wild beasts which he had provided for a gladiatorial show were rather costly, he selected criminals to be devoured, and reviewing the line of prisoners without examining the charges, but merely taking his place in the middle of a colonnade, he bade them be led away "from baldhead to baldhead." 2 A man who had made a vow to fight in the arena, if the emperor recovered, he compelled to keep his word, watched him as he fought sword in hand, and would not let him go until he was victorious, and then only after many entreaties. Another who had offered his life for the same reason, but delayed to kill himself, he turned over to his slaves, with orders to drive him through the streets decked with sacred boughs and fillets, calling for the fulfilment of his vow, and finally hurl him from the embankment. 3 Many men of honourable rank were first disfigured with the marks of branding-irons and then condemned to the mines, to work at building roads, or to be thrown to the wild beasts; or else he shut them up in cages on all fours, like animals, or had them sawn asunder. Not all these punishments were for serious offences, but merely for criticising one of his shows, or for never having sworn by his Genius. 4 He forced parents to attend the executions of their sons, sending a litter for one man who pleaded ill health, and inviting another to dinner immediately after witnessing the death, and trying to rouse him to gaiety and jesting by a great show of affability. He had the manager of his gladiatorial shows and beast-baitings beaten with chains in his presence for several successive days, and would not kill him until he was disgusted at the stench of his putrefied brain. He burned a writer of Atellan farces alive in the middle of the arena of the amphitheatre, because of a humorous line of double meaning. When a Roman knight on being thrown to the wild beasts loudly protested his innocence, he took him out, cut off his tongue, and put him back again.

28  1 Having asked a man who had been recalled from an exile of long standing, how in the world he spent his time there, the man replied by way of flattery: "I constantly prayed the gods for what has come to pass, that Tiberius might die and you become emperor." Thereupon Caligula, thinking that his exiles were likewise praying for his death, sent emissaries from island to island to butcher them all. Wishing to have one of the senators torn to pieces, he induced some

of the members to assail him suddenly, on his entrance into the House, with the charge of being a public enemy, to stab him with their •styles, and turn him over to the rest to be mangled; and his cruelty was not sated until he saw the man's limbs, members, and bowels dragged through the streets and heaped up before him.

29  1 He added to the enormity of his crimes by the brutality of his language. He used to say that there was nothing in his own character which he admired and approved more highly than what he called his ἀδιατρεψία, that is to say, his shameless impudence. When his grandmother Antonia gave him some advice, he was not satisfied merely to listen but replied: "Remember that I have the right to do anything to anybody." When he was on the point of killing his brother, and suspected that he had taken drugs as a precaution against poison, he cried: "What! an antidote against Caesar?" After banishing his sisters, he made the threat that he not only had islands, but swords as well. 2 An ex-praetor who had retired to Anticyra for his health, sent frequent requests for an extension of his leave, but Caligula had him put to death, adding that a man who had not been helped by so long a course of hellebore needed to be bled. On signing the list of prisoners who were to be put to death later, he said that he was clearing his accounts. Having condemned several Gauls and Greeks to death in a body, he boasted that he had subdued Gallograecia.

30  1 He seldom had anyone put to death except by numerous slight wounds, his constant order, which soon became well-known, being: "Strike so that he may feel that he is dying." When a different man than he had intended had been killed, through a mistake in the names, he said that the victim too had deserved the same fate. He often uttered the familiar line of the tragic poet:

"Let them hate me, so they but fear me."

2 He often inveighed against all the senators alike, as adherents of Sejanus and informers against his mother and brothers, producing the documents which he pretended to have burned, and upholding the cruelty of Tiberius as forced upon him, since he could not but believe so many accusers. He constantly tongue-lashed the equestrian order as devotees of the stage and the arena. Angered at the rabble for applauding a faction which he opposed, he cried: "I wish the Roman people had but a single neck," and when the brigand Tetrinius was demanded, he said that those who asked for him were Tetriniuses also. 3 Once a band of five retiarii in tunics, matched against the same number of secutores, yielded without a struggle; but when their death was ordered, one of them caught up his trident and slew all the victors. Caligula bewailed this in a public proclamation as a most cruel murder, and expressed his horror of those who had had the heart to

witness it.

31   1 He even used openly to deplore the state of his times, because they had been marked by no public disasters, saying that the rule of Augustus had been made famous by the Varus massacre, and that of Tiberius by the collapse of the amphitheatre at Fidenae, while his own was threatened with oblivion because of its prosperity; and every now and then he wished for the destruction of his armies, for famine, pestilence, fires, or a great earthquake.

32   1 His acts and words were equally cruel, even when he was indulging in relaxation and given up to amusement and feasting. While he was lunching or revelling capital examinations by torture were often made in his presence, and a soldier who was adept at decapitation cut off the heads of those who were brought from prison. At Puteoli, at the dedication of the bridge that he contrived, as has been said, after inviting a number to come to him from the shore, on a sudden he had them all thrown overboard; and when some caught hold of the rudders of the ships, he pushed them off into the sea with boathooks and oars. 2 At a public banquet in Rome he immediately handed a slave over to the executioners for stealing a strip of silver from the couches, with orders that his hands be cut off and hung from his neck upon his breast, and that he then be led about among the guests, preceded by a placard giving the reason for his punishment. When a murmillo from the gladiatorial school fought with him with wooden swords and fell on purpose, he stabbed him with a real dagger and then ran about with a palm-branch, as victors do. 3 Once when he stood by the altar dressed as a popa, and a victim was brought up, he raised his mallet on high and slew the cultrarius. At one of his more sumptuous banquets he suddenly burst into a fit of laughter, and when the consuls, who were reclining next him, politely inquired at what he was laughing, he replied; "What do you suppose, except that at a single nod of mine both of you could have your throats cut on the spot?"

33   1 As a sample of his humour, he took his place beside a statue of Jupiter, and asked the tragic actor Apelles which of the two seemed to him the greater, and when he hesitated, Caligula had him flayed with whips, extolling his voice from time to time, when the wretch begged for mercy, as passing sweet even in his groans. Whenever he kissed the neck of his wife or sweetheart, he would say: "Off comes this beautiful head whenever I give the word." He even used to threaten now and then that he would resort to torture if necessary, to find out from his dear Caesonia why he loved her so passionately.

34  1 He assailed mankind of almost every epoch with no less envy and malice than insolence and cruelty. He threw down the statues of famous men, which for lack of room Augustus had moved from the court of the Capitol to the Campus Martius, and so utterly demolished them that they could not be set up again with their inscriptions entire; and thereafter he forbade the erection of the statue of any living man anywhere, without his knowledge and consent. 2 He even thought of destroying the poems of Homer, asking why he should not have the same privilege as Plato, who excluded Homer from his ideal commonwealth. More than that, he all but removed the writings and the busts of Vergil and of Titus Livius from all the libraries, railing at the former as a man of no literary talent and very little learning, and the latter as a verbose and careless historian. With regard to lawyers too, as if intending to do away with any practice of their profession, he often threatened that he would see to it, by Heaven, that they could give no advice contrary to his wish.

35  1 He took from all the noblest of the city the ancient devices of their families, from Torquatus his collar, from Cincinnatus his lock of hair, from Gnaeus Pompeius the surname Great belonging to his ancient race. After inviting Ptolemy, whom I have mentioned before, to come from his kingdom and receiving him with honour, he suddenly had him executed for no other reason than that when giving a gladiatorial show, he noticed that Ptolemy on entering the theatre attracted general attention by the splendour of his purple cloak. 2 Whenever he ran across handsome men with fine heads of hair, he disfigured them by having the backs of their heads shaved. There was a certain Aesius Proculus, son of a chief centurion, called Colosseros because of his remarkable size and handsome appearance; this man Caligula ordered to be suddenly dragged from his seat in the amphitheatre and led into the arena, where he matched him first against a Thracian and then against a heavy-armed gladiator; when Proculus was victor in both contests, Caligula gave orders that he be bound at once, clad in rags, and then put to death, after first being led about the streets and exhibited to the women. 3 In short, there was no one of such low condition or such abject fortune that he did not envy him such advantages as he possessed. Since the king of Nemi had now held his priesthood for many years, he hired a stronger adversary to attack him. When an essedarius called Porius was vigorously applauded on the day of one of the games for setting his slave free after a victory, Caligula rushed from the amphitheatre in such haste that he trod on the fringe of his toga and went headlong down the steps, fuming and shouting: "The people that rule the world give more honour to a gladiator for a trifling act than to their deified emperors or to the one still present with them."

36  1 He respected neither his own chastity nor that of anyone else. He is said to have had unnatural relations with Marcus Lepidus, the pantomimic actor Mnester, and certain hostages. Valerius Catullus, a young man of a consular family, publicly proclaimed that he had violated

the emperor and worn himself out in commerce with him. To say nothing of his incest with his sisters and his notorious passion for the concubine Pyrallis, there was scarcely any woman of rank whom he did not approach. 2 These as a rule he invited to dinner with their husbands, and as they passed by the foot of his couch, he would inspect them critically and deliberately, as if buying slaves, even putting out his hand and lifting up the face of anyone who looked down in modesty; then as often as the fancy took him he would leave the room, sending for the one who pleased him best, and returning soon afterwards with evident signs of what had occurred, he would openly commend or criticise his partner, recounting her charms or defects and commenting on her conduct. To some he personally sent a bill of divorce in the name of their absent husbands, and had it entered in the public records.

37　1 In reckless extravagance he outdid the prodigals of all times in ingenuity, inventing a new sort of baths and unnatural varieties of food and feasts; for he would bathe in hot or cold perfumed oils, drink pearls of great price dissolved in vinegar, and set before his guests loaves and meats of gold, declaring that a man ought either to be frugal or Caesar. He even scattered large sums of money among the commons from the roof of the basilica Julia for several days in succession. 2 He also built Liburnian galleys with ten banks of oars, with sterns set with gems, particoloured sails, huge spacious baths, colonnades, and banquet-halls, and even a great variety of vines and fruit trees; that on board of them he might recline at table from an early hour, and coast along the shores of Campania amid songs and choruses. He built villas and country houses with utter disregard of expense, caring for nothing so much as to do what men said was impossible. 3 So he built moles out into the deep and stormy sea, tunnelled rocks of hardest flint, built up plains to the height of mountains and razed mountains to the level of the plain; all with incredible dispatch, since the penalty for delay was death. To make a long story short, vast sums of money, including the 2,700,000,000 sesterces which Tiberius Caesar had amassed, were squandered by him in less than the revolution of a year.

38　1 Having thus impoverished himself, from very need he turned his attention to pillage through a complicated and cunningly devised system of false accusations, auction sales, and imposts. He ruled that Roman citizenship could not lawfully be enjoyed by those whose forefathers had obtained it for themselves and their descendants, except in the case of sons, since "descendants" ought not to be understood as going beyond that degree; and when certificates of the deified Julius and Augustus were presented to him, he waved them aside as old and out of date. 2 He also charged that those estates had been falsely returned, to which any addition had later been made from any cause whatever. If any chief centurions since the beginning of Tiberius' reign had not named that emperor or himself among their heirs, he set aside their wills on the ground of ingratitude; also the testaments of all others, as null and void, if anyone had said that they had intended to make Caesar their heir when they died. When he had roused such fear in this way that he came to be named openly as heir by strangers among their intimates and by parents among their children, he accused them of making game of him by continuing to live after such a declaration, and to many of them he sent poisoned dainties. 3 He used further to conduct the trial of such cases in person, naming in advance the sum which he proposed to raise at each sitting, and not rising until it was made up. Impatient of the slightest delay, he once condemned in a single sentence more than forty who were accused on different counts, boasting to Caesonia, when she woke after a nap, of the great amount of business he had done while she was taking her siesta.

4 Appointing an auction, he put up and sold what was left from all the shows, personally soliciting bids and running them up so high, that some who were forced to buy articles at an enormous price and were thus stripped of their possessions, opened their veins. A well-known incident is that of Aponius Saturninus; he fell asleep on one of the benches, and as the auctioneer was warned by Gaius not to overlook praetorian gentleman who kept nodding to him, the bidding was not stopped until thirteen gladiators were knocked down to the unconscious sleeper at nine million sesterces.

39   1 When he was in Gaul and had sold at immense figures the jewels, furniture, slaves, and even the freedmen of his sisters who had been condemned to death, finding the business so profitable, he sent to the city for all the paraphernalia of the old palace, seizing for its transportation even public carriages and animals from the bakeries; with the result that bread was often scarce at Rome and many who had cases in court lost them from inability to appear and meet their bail. 2 To get rid of this furniture, he resorted to every kind of trickery and wheedling, now railing at the bidders for avarice and because they were not ashamed to be richer than he, and now feigning regret for allowing common men to acquire the property of princes. Having learned that a rich provincial had paid those who issued the emperor's invitations two hundred thousand sesterces, to be smuggled in among the guests at one of his dinner-parties, he was not in the least displeased that the honour of dining with him was rated so high; but when next day the man appeared at his auction, he sent a messenger to hand him some trifle or other at the price of two hundred thousand sesterces and say that he should dine with Caesar on his personal invitation.

40   1 He levied new and unheard of taxes, at first through the publicans and then, because their profit was so great, through the centurions and tribunes of the praetorian guard;f and there was no class of commodities or men on which he did not impose some form of tariff. On all eatables

sold in any part of the city he levied a fixed and definite charge; on lawsuits and legal processes begun anywhere, a fortieth part of the sum involved, providing a penalty in case anyone was found guilty of compromising or abandoning a suit; on the daily wages of porters, an eighth; on the earnings of prostitutes, as much as each received for one embrace;g and a clause was added to this chapter of the law, providing that those who had ever been prostitutes or acted as panders should be liable to this public tax, and that even matrimony should not be exempt.

41  1 When taxes of this kind had been proclaimed, but not published in writing, inasmuch as many offences were committed through ignorance of the letter of the law, he at last, on the urgent demand of the people, had the law posted up, but in a very narrow place and in excessively small letters, to prevent the making of a copy. To leave no kind of plunder untried, he opened a brothel in his palace, setting apart a number of rooms and furnishing them to suit the grandeur of the place, where matrons and freeborn youths should stand exposed. Then he sent his pages about the fora and basilicas, to invite young men and old to enjoy themselves, lending money on interest to those who came and having clerks openly take down their names, as contributors to Caesar's revenues. 2 He did not even disdain to make money from play, and to increase his gains by falsehood and even by perjury. Having on one occasion given up his place to the player next to him and gone into the courtyard, he spied two wealthy Roman knights passing by; he ordered them to be seized at once and their property confiscated and came back exultant, boasting that he had never played in better luck.

42  1 But when his daughter was born, complaining of his narrow means, and no longer merely of the burdens of a ruler but of those of a father as well, he took up contributions for the girl's maintenance and dowry. He also made proclamation that he would receive New Year's gifts, and on the Kalends of January took his place in the entrance to the Palace, to clutch the coins which a throng of people of all classes showered on him by handfuls and lapfuls. Finally, seized with a mania for feeling the touch of money, he would often pour out huge piles of goldpieces in some open place, walk over them barefooted, and wallow in them for a long time with his whole body.

43  1 He had but one experience with military affairs or war, and then on a sudden impulse; for having gone to Mevania to visit the river Clitumnus and its grove, he was reminded of the necessity of recruiting his body-guard of Batavians and was seized with the idea of an expedition to Germany. So without delay he assembled legions and auxiliaries from all quarters, holding levies everywhere with the utmost strictness, and collecting provisions of every kind on an unheard of scale. Then he began his march and made it now so hurriedly and rapidly, that the

praetorian cohorts were forced, contrary to all precedent, to lay their standards on the pack-animals and thus to follow him; again he was so lazy and luxurious that he was carried in a litter by eight bearers, requiring the inhabitants of the towns through which he passed to sweep the roads for him and sprinkle them to lay the dust.

44   1 On reaching his camp, to show his vigilance and strictness as a commander, he dismissed in disgrace the generals who were late in bringing in the auxiliaries from various places, and in reviewing his troops he deprived many of the chief centurions who were well on in years of their rank, in some cases only a few days before they would have served their time, giving as a reason their age and infirmity; then railing at the rest for their avarice, he reduced the rewards given on completion of full military service to six thousand sesterces.

2 All that he accomplished was to receive the surrender of Adminius, son of Cynobellinus king of the Britons, who had been banished by his father and had deserted to the Romans with a small force; yet as if the entire island had submitted to him, he sent a grandiloquent letter to Rome, commanding the couriers who carried it to ride in their post-chaise all the way to the Forum and the House, and not to deliver it to anyone except the consuls, in the temple of Mars the Avenger, before a full meeting of the senate.

45   1 Presently, finding no one to fight with, he had a few Germans of his body-guard taken across the river and concealed there, and word brought him after luncheon with great bustle and confusion that the enemy were close at hand. Upon this he rushed out with his friends and a part of the praetorian cavalry to the woods close by, and after cutting the branches from some trees and adorning them like trophies, he returned by torchlight, taunting those who had not followed him as timorous and cowardly, and presenting his companions and the partners in his victory with crowns of a new kind and of a new name, ornamented with figures of the sun, moon and stars, and called exploratoriae. 2 Another time some hostages were taken from a common school and secretly sent on ahead of him, when he suddenly left a banquet and pursued them with the cavalry as if they were runaways, caught them, and brought them back in fetters, in this farce too showing immoderate extravagance. On coming back to the table, when some announced that the army was assembled, he urged them to take their places just as they were, in their coats of mail. He also admonished them in the familiar line of Vergil to "bear up and save themselves for better days."

3 Meanwhile he rebuked the absent senate and people in a stern edict because "while Caesar was fighting and exposed to such dangers they were indulging in revels and frequenting the theatres and their pleasant villas."

46   1 Finally, as if he intended to bring the war to an end, he drew up a line of battle on the shore of the Ocean, arranging his ballistas and other artillery; and when no one knew or could imagine what he was going to do, he suddenly bade them gather shells and fill their helmets and the folds of their gowns, calling them "spoils from the Ocean, due to the Capitol and Palatine." As a monument of his victory he erected a lofty tower, from which lights were to shine at night to guide the course of ships, as from the Pharos. Then promising the soldiers a gratuity of a hundred denarii each, as if he had shown unprecedented liberality, he said, "Go your way happy; go your way rich."

47   1 Then turning his attention to his triumph, in addition to a few captives and deserters from the barbarians he chose all the tallest of the Gauls, and as he expressed it, those who were "worthy of a triumph," as well as some of the chiefs. These he reserved for his parade, compelling them not only to dye their hair red and to let it grow long, but also to learn the language of the Germans and assume barbarian names. He also had the triremes in which he had entered the Ocean carried overland to Rome for the greater part of the way. He wrote besides to his financial agents to prepare for a triumph at the smallest possible cost, but on a grander scale than had ever before been known, since the goods of all were at their disposal.

48   1 Before leaving the province he formed a design of unspeakable cruelty, that of butchering the legions that had begun the mutiny years before just after the death of Augustus, because they had beleaguered° his father Germanicus, their leader, and himself, at the time an infant; and though he was with difficulty turned from this mad purpose, he could by no means be prevented from persisting in his desire to decimate them. Accordingly he summoned them to an assembly without their arms, not even wearing their swords, and surrounded them with armed horsemen. 2 But seeing that some of the legionaries, suspecting his purpose, were stealing off to resume their arms, in case any violence should be offered them, he fled from the assembly and set out for the city in a hurry, turning all his ferocity upon the senate, against which he uttered open threats, in order to divert the gossip about his own dishonour. He complained among other things that he had been cheated of his fairly earned triumph; whereas a short time before he had himself given orders that on pain of death no action should be taken about his honours.

49  1 Therefore when he was met on the road by envoys from that distinguished body, begging him to hasten his return, he roared, "I will come, and this will be with me," frequently smiting the hilt of the sword which he wore at his side. He also made proclamation that he was returning, but only to those who desired his presence, the equestrian order and the people, for to the senate he would never more be fellow-citizen nor prince. 2 He even forbade anyone of the senators to meet him. Then giving up or postponing his triumph, he entered the city on his birthday in an ovation; and within four months he perished, having dared great crimes and meditating still greater ones. For he had made up his mind to move to Antium, and later to Alexandria, after first slaying the noblest members of the two orders. 3 That no one may doubt this, let me say that among his private papers two notebooks were found with different titles, one called "The Sword" and the other "The Dagger," and both containing the names and marks of identification of those whom he had doomed to death. There was found besides a great chest full of divers kinds of poisons, which they say were later thrown into the sea by Claudius and so infected it as to kill the fish, which were thrown up by the tide upon the neighbouring shores.

50  1 He was very tall and extremely pale, with an unshapely body, but very thin neck and legs. His eyes and temples were hollow, his forehead broad and grim, his hair thin and entirely gone on the top of his head, though his body was hairy. Because of this to look upon him from a higher place as he passed by, or for any reason whatever to mention a goat, was treated as a capital offence. While his face was naturally forbidding and ugly, he purposely made it even more savage, practising all kinds of terrible and fearsome expressions before a mirror.

2 He was sound neither of body nor mind. As a boy he was troubled with the falling sickness, and while in his youth he had some endurance, yet at times because of sudden faintness he was hardly able to walk, to stand up, to collect his thoughts, or to hold up his head. He himself realised his mental infirmity, and thought at times of going into retirement and clearing his brain. It is thought that his wife Caesonia gave him a drug intended for a love potion, which however had the effect of driving him mad. 3 He was especially tormented with sleeplessness; for he never rested more than three hours at night, and even for that length of time he did not sleep quietly, but was terrified by strange apparitions, once for example dreaming that the spirit of the Ocean talked with him. Therefore weary of lying in bed wide awake during the greater part of the night, he would now sit upon his couch, and now wander through the long colonnades, crying out from time to time for daylight and longing for its coming.

51  1 I think I may fairly attribute to mental weakness the existence of two exactly opposite faults in the same person, extreme assurance and, on the other hand, excessive timorousness. For

this man, who so utterly despised the gods, was wont at the slightest thunder and lightning to shut his eyes, to muffle up his head, and if they increased, to leap from his bed and hide under it. In his journey through Sicily, though he made all manner of fun of the miracles in various places, he suddenly fled from Messana by night, panic-stricken by the smoke and roaring from Aetna's crater. 2 Full of threats as he was also against the barbarians, when he was riding in a chariot through a narrow defile on the far side of the Rhine, and someone said that there would be no slight panic if the enemy should appear anywhere, he immediately mounted a horse and hastily returned to the bridges. Finding them crowded with camp servants and baggage, in his impatience of any delay he was passed along from hand to hand over the men's heads. 3 Soon after, hearing of an uprising in Germany, he made preparations to flee from the city and equipped fleets for the purpose, finding comfort only in the thought that the provinces across the sea would at any rate be left him, in case the enemy should be victorious and take possession of the summits of the Alps, as the Cimbri, or even of the city, as the Senones had once done. And it was this, I think, that later inspired his assassins with the idea of pretending to the riotous soldiers that he had laid hands on himself in terror at the report of a defeat.

52   1 In his clothing, his shoes, and the rest of his attire he did not follow the usage of his country and his fellow-citizens; not always even that of his sex; or in fact, that of an ordinary mortal. He often appeared in public in embroidered cloaks covered with precious stones, with a long-sleeved tunic and bracelets; sometimes in silk and in a woman's robe; now in slippers or buskins, again in boots, such as the emperor's body-guard wear, and at times in the low shoes which are used by females. But oftentimes he exhibited himself with a golden beard, holding in his hand a thunderbolt, a trident, or a caduceus, emblems of the gods, and even in the garb of Venus. He frequently wore the dress of a triumphing general, even before his campaign, and sometimes the breastplate of Alexander the Great, which he had taken from his sarcophagus.

53   1 As regards liberal studies, he gave little attention to literature but a great deal to oratory, and he was as ready of speech and eloquent as you please, especially if he had occasion to make a charge against anyone. For when he was angry, he had an abundant flow of words and thoughts, and his voice and delivery were such that for very excitement he could not stand still and he was clearly heard by those at a distance. 2 When about to begin an harangue, he threatened to draw the sword of his nightly labours, and he had such scorn of a polished and elegant style that he used to say that Seneca, who was very popular just then, composed "mere school exercises," and that he was "sand without lime." He had the habit of writing replies to the successful pleas of orators and composing accusations and defences of important personages who were brought to trial before the senate; and according as his pen had run most easily, he brought ruin or relief to each of them by his speech, while he would also invite the equestrian

order by proclamation to come in and hear him.

54   1 Moreover he devoted himself with much enthusiasm to arts of other kinds and of great variety, appearing as a Thracian gladiator, as a charioteer, and even as a singer and dancer, fighting with the weapons of actual warfare, and driving in circuses built in various places; so carried away by his interest in singing and dancing that even at the public performances he could not refrain from singing with the tragic actor as he delivered his lines, or from openly imitating his gestures by way of praise or correction. 2 Indeed, on the day when he was slain he seems to have ordered an all-night vigil for the sole purpose of taking advantage of the licence of the occasion to make his first appearance on the stage. Sometimes he danced even at night, and once he summoned three consulars to the Palace at the close of the second watch, and when they arrived in great and deathly fear, he seated them on a stage and then on a sudden burst out with a great din of flutes and clogs, dressed in a cloak and a tunic reaching to his heels, and after dancing a number went off again. And yet varied as were his accomplishments, the man could not swim.

55   1 Toward those to whom he was devoted his partiality became madness. He used to kiss Mnester, an actor of pantomimes, even in the theatre, and if anyone made even the slightest sound while his favourite was dancing, he had him dragged from his seat and scourged him with his own hand. When a Roman knight created a disturbance, he sent a centurion to bid him go without delay to Ostia and carry a message for him to king Ptolemy in Mauretania; and its purport was this: "Do neither good nor ill to the man whom I have sent you." 2 He gave some Thracian gladiators command of his German body-guard. He reduced the amount of armour of the murmillones. When one Columbus had won a victory, but had suffered from a slight wound, he had the place rubbed with a poison which he henceforth called "Columbinum"; at least that name was found included in his list of poisons. He was so passionately devoted to the green faction that he constantly dined and spent the night in their stable, and in one of his revels with them he gave the driver Eutychus two million sesterces in gifts. 3 He used to send his soldiers on the day before the games and order silence in the neighbourhood, to prevent the horse Incitatus from being disturbed. Besides a stall of marble, a manger of ivory, purple blankets and a collar of precious stones, he even gave this horse a house, a troop of slaves and furniture, for the more elegant entertainment of the guests invited in his name; and it is also said that he planned to make him consul.

56   1 During this frantic and riotous career several thought of attempting his life. But when one or two conspiracies had been detected and the rest were waiting for a favourable opportunity,

two men made common cause and succeeded, with the connivance of his most influential freedmen and the officers of the praetorian guard; for although the charge that these last were privy to one of the former conspiracies was false, they realised that Caligula hated and feared them. In fact, he exposed them to great odium by at once taking them aside and declaring, drawn sword in hand, that he would kill himself, if they too thought he deserved death; and from that time on he never ceased accusing them one to the other and setting them all at odds.

2 When they had decided to attempt his life at the exhibition of the Palatine games, as he went out at noon, Cassius Chaerea, tribune of a cohort of the praetorian guard, claimed for himself the principal part; for Gaius used to taunt him, a man already well on in years, with voluptuousness and effeminacy by every form of insult. When he asked for the watchword Gaius would give him "Priapus" or "Venus," and when Chaerea had occasion to thank him for anything, he would hold out his hand to kiss, forming and moving it in an obscene fashion.

57　1 His approaching murder was foretold by many prodigies. The statue of Jupiter at Olympia, which he had ordered to be taken to pieces and moved to Rome, suddenly uttered such a peal of laughter that the scaffoldings collapsed and the workmen took to their heels; and at once a man called Cassius turned up, who declared that he had been bidden in a dream to sacrifice a bull to Jupiter. 2 The Capitol at Capua was struck by lightning on the Ides of March, and also the room of the doorkeeper of the Palace at Rome. Some inferred from the latter omen that danger was threatened to the owner at the hands of his guards; and from the former, the murder of a second distinguished personage, such as had taken place long before on that same day. The soothsayer Sulla too, when Gaius consulted him about his horoscope, declared that inevitable death was close at hand. 3 The lots of Fortune at Antium warned him to beware of Cassius, and he accordingly ordered the death of Cassius Longinus, who was at the time proconsul of Asia, forgetting that the family name of Chaerea was Cassius. The day before he was killed he dreamt that he stood in heaven beside the throne of Jupiter and that the god struck him with the toe of his right foot and hurled him to earth. Some things which had happened on that very day shortly before he was killed were also regarded as portents. 4 As he was sacrificing, he was sprinkled with the blood of a flamingo, and the pantomimic actor Mnester danced a tragedy which the tragedian Neoptolemus had acted years before during the games at which Philip king of the Macedonians was assassinated. In a farce called "Laureolus," in which the chief actor falls as he is making his escape and vomits blood, several understudies so vied with one another in giving evidence of their proficiency that the stage swam in blood. A nocturnal performance besides was rehearsing, in which scenes from the lower world were represented by Egyptians and Aethiopians.

58  1 On the ninth day before the Kalends of February at about the seventh hour he hesitated whether or not to get up for luncheon, since his stomach was still disordered from excess of food on the day before, but at length he came out at the persuasion of his friends. In the covered passage through which he had to pass, some boys of good birth, who had been summoned from Asia to appear on the stage, were rehearsing their parts, and he stopped to watch and to encourage them; and had not the leader of the troop complained that he had a chill, he would have returned and had the performance given at once. 2 From this point there are two versions of the story: some say that as he was talking with the boys, Chaerea came up behind, and gave him a deep cut in the neck, having first cried, "Take that," and that then the tribune Cornelius Sabinus, who was the other conspirator and faced Gaius, stabbed him in the breast. Others say that Sabinus, after getting rid of the crowd through centurions who were in the plot, asked for the watchword, as soldiers do, and that when Gaius gave him "Jupiter," he cried "So be it," and as Gaius looked around, he split his jawbone with a blow of his sword. 3 As he lay upon the ground and with writhing limbs called out that he still lived, the others dispatched him with thirty wounds; for the general signal was "Strike again." Some even thrust their swords through his privates. At the beginning of the disturbance his bearers ran to his aid with their poles, and presently the Germans of his body-guard, and they slew several of his assassins, as well as some inoffensive senators.

59  1 He lived twenty-nine years and ruled three years, ten months and eight days. His body was conveyed secretly to the gardens of the Lamian family, where it was partly consumed on a hastily erected pyre and buried beneath a light covering of turf; later his sisters on their return from exile dug it up, cremated it, and consigned it to the tomb. Before this was done, it is well known that the caretakers of the gardens were disturbed by ghosts, and that in the house where he was slain not a night passed without some fearsome apparition,h until at last the house itself was destroyed by fire. With him died his wife Caesonia, stabbed with a sword by a centurion, while his daughter's brains were dashed out against a wall.

60  1 One may form an idea of the state of those times by what followed. Not even after the murder was made known was it at once believed that he was dead, but it was suspected that Gaius himself had made up and circulated the report, to find out by that means how men felt towards him. The conspirators too had not agreed on a successor, and the senate was so unanimously in favour of re-establishing the republic that the consuls called the first meeting, not in the senate house, because it had the name Julia, but in the Capitol; while some in expressing their views proposed that the memory of the Caesars be done away with and their temples destroyed. Men further observed and commented on the fact that all the Caesars whose forename was Gaius perished by the sword, beginning with the one who was slain in the times of Cinna.

**Bibliography**

**Ancient Works:**

Cassius Dio, *Roman History, Book 59*

Josephus, *Antiquities of the Jews*, Books XVIII–XIX

Philo of Alexandria, *On the Embassy to Gaius*

Seneca the Younger

Suetonius, *The Lives of Twelve Caesars*, Life of Caligula

**Modern Works:**

Balsdon, V. D. (1934). *The Emperor Gaius.*

Barrett, Anthony A. (1989). *Caligula: the corruption of power.*

Grant, Michael (1979). *The Twelve Caesars.*

Hurley, Donna W. (1993). *An Historical and Historiographical Commentary on Suetonius' Life of C. Caligula.*

# Nero

### Chapter 1: Nero's Early Life and Rise to Power, 37-54 A.D.

Like all of the members of the Julio-Claudian dynasty, of which he was the last, Nero (born Lucius Domitius Ahenobarbus) could boast a pedigree that put even the noblest of Roman families to shame. His father was Gnaeus Domitius Ahenobarbus, great-nephew to Octavian (Caesar Augustus), second cousin to Caligula, and cousin to Claudius, while his mother was Agrippina the Younger, great-grand-daughter of Augustus and sister to Caligula. Through both of them, Nero was also related to Tiberius, Mark Antony, and Marcus Agrippa.

Though the parentage of Nero's mother and father might be distinguished, their character was markedly less so. By all accounts Gnaeus Ahenobarbus was a despicable man, with several stories demonstrating his evil. According to ancient historians, he is supposed to have murdered one of his freedmen for refusing to participate in a drinking contest, he was accused of deliberately running down a child playing in the street with his chariot, and he allegedly plucked the eye out of a Roman nobleman's skull for criticising him in public. He was also a cheat, a liar, an inveterate gambler, a corrupt politician, a serial womaniser, and if the accusations brought against him by Emperor Tiberius are to be believed, an incestuous adulterer. Tiberius would have gladly prosecuted him for these crimes, but he died prematurely before having the chance to do so.

**Aureus of Nero and his mother, Agrippina, circa 54**

Nero's mother Agrippina, whom Gnaeus married when she was 13 (Gnaeus was 45 at the time), concealed beneath an outwardly sweet and charming demeanour a nature as warm and appealing as a snake's. Her incessant scheming for power, in addition to her penchant for seducing high-placed lovers (including, if Cassius Dio is to be believed, her brother Caligula) would play a major part in Nero's life, and obviously not in a positive manner. Anyone with even a basic understanding of psychiatry would conclude that, with parents such as this choice pair, Nero never stood a chance, and they would not be wrong. Certainly having two such influences overshadowing his formative years cannot have helped, and even Gnaeus himself was said to remark – or to boast – that any child of his and Agrippina's was guaranteed to both be detestable and, should he ever hold any form of public office, a genuine threat to Rome.

**Bust of Agrippina the Younger**

Nero was born in Antium, a coastal town a few miles from Rome, on December 15$^{th}$, 37 A.D., during the reign of Caligula, who had taken the throne in March of 37 A.D. after Tiberius's death. Rumour was rampant that Caligula was having an incestuous relationship with Agrippina, as well as with his sisters Drusilla and Livilla, but this seems not to have troubled Gnaeus – possibly because he was already sickening with the dropsy (edema) which carried him off, in exquisite pain, in 39 A.D., when Nero was two. That same year, Agrippina became involved in what became known as the Plot of the Three Daggers, a conspiracy to murder Caligula and put Marcus Lepidus, Drusilla's husband, on the throne. The main architects of the plot were Lepidus himself, alongside Agrippina and Livilla – Drusilla had died the year before, and since she was Caligula's favourite, the other two sisters had swiftly found themselves in disfavour.

**Caligula**

The plot, however, was swiftly discovered. Caligula had Lepidus put to death and banished Agrippina and Livilla to the Pontine islands, after stripping them from their estates. Nero, who was set to inherit his father's wealth, found himself dispossessed by Caligula, and was sent to live with his aunt Domitia the Younger.

In 41 B.C., Caligula was murdered by the Praetorian Guard along with his wife and his daughter (whom he had disturbingly named after Drusilla). In his place, the Praetorians and the Roman aristocracy selected the more pliable (and less insane) Claudius, Agrippina's uncle. Claudius had been afflicted by an illness early in life that left him slightly deaf with a limp and a stutter, maladies that may have saved his life. With Claudius viewed as such a pathetic figure, he was not perceived as much of a threat or enemy in Rome, and his physical defects had led him to spend much of his free time reading and becoming educated. Claudius came to be considered one of Rome's most competent early emperors, helped no doubt by the fact that he was sandwiched inbetween Caligula and Nero.

**Bust of Claudius**

Claudius, who was notoriously tolerant, ended Agrippina's exile along with Livilla's, though by all accounts he – and Nero – would have been better off if he had left her on the Pontine islands to rot. While Livilla retired to private life, Agrippina, after being reunited with Nero, who was four at the time, began to attempt to seduce any highly placed individual she could lay her hands upon. She was rebuffed by the future emperor Galba, but her advances were so shameless that they led to Galba's wife publicly slapping her in the face in the forum.

Another man, however, was not immune to her arts. This was Gaius Sallustius Crispus, the husband of Nero's aunt Domitia the Elder (not to be confused with his other aunt Domitia the Younger, who had cared for him during Agrippina's exile). By all accounts, Crispus was a genial, literate, clever and wealthy man, and he divorced Domitia in order to be with Agrippina, who became his wife shortly thereafter. Agrippina now contrived to keep her political profile to a bare minimum, in order to avoid attracting notice from Claudius's new wife, the notorious Messalina, who was her second cousin. Messalina had succeeded in discrediting Livilla by accusing her of adultery with Seneca (who would later become Nero's tutor), and even went so far as to attempt to have Nero murdered as he was taking an afternoon nap. The assassins she sent to murder him, however, mistook a sloughed-off snakeskin protruding from his pillow (which Nero had likely collected as a souvenir) for a genuine snake, and fled in terror.

**Statue of Nero and Seneca**

**Statue of Messalini and son Brittanicus in the Louvre**

In 47 A.D., six years after he had first married Agrippina, Crispus died under mysterious circumstances, by all accounts poisoned by Agrippina. Crispus, who was extremely wealthy, left his vast estates to Nero, who was – conveniently – too young to administer them himself. His guardian, of course, was Agrippina herself.

Flush with his wealth, Agrippina now felt confident enough to challenge Messalina, and she attended a pageant with the 10 year old Nero, who was applauded by the people far more then Messalina's son, Britannicus. The public was sympathetic to the exiled widow's plight, while Messalina's excesses were well known. The following year, Messalina was implicated in a plot to murder Claudius and set one of her lovers in his place, and Claudius had her executed.

For an ambitious woman with no morals like Agrippina, this was a heaven-sent chance, particularly as it was rumoured that Claudius was notorious for being easily swayed by his wives. Agrippina promptly became the mistress of Marcus Pallas, one of Claudius's influential freedmen, who then persuaded Claudius to marry her. Agrippina had a large part in this, since she actively worked to seduce the weak-willed Claudius, and in 49 A.D. they were married. Claudius presented the marriage as one in the public interest, since (understandably) a marriage between uncle and niece was considered incest and impious even then. Despite widespread public disapproval and outcry, the marriage went ahead, and Agrippina was now the most powerful woman in the Empire.

She was also taking steps to ensure both her political survival and Nero's future, for she was desperate to have him inherit the throne. Agrippina's rivals were accused of any number of false crimes, and either driven into exile, executed, or quietly murdered, and she managed to coerce Claudius into disowning Britannicus, who was next in line to the throne. In 50 B.C., Claudius formally adopted the 13 year old Nero as his son, granting him the name Nero Claudius Caesar Drusus Germanicus.

**Coin issued under Claudius celebrating young Nero as the future emperor, circa 50**

A year afterwards, Nero donned the *toga virilis* at the age of 14 and was officially declared a man. He was granted the title of proconsul by Claudius and made his first public appearance before the Senate, following which honour he was displayed on coinage alongside his adoptive father. Two years later, in 53 A.D., Nero married his step-sister, Claudia Octavia.

**Coin depicting Claudia Octavia**

In all likelihood, it is around this time that Nero began to resent being a mere pawn in his mother's struggle for power, although he remained largely under her spell. He also had cause to thank her when, in 54 A.D., Claudius died. According to many ancient historians, it was Agrippina herself who was responsible for his death, for she is said to have murdered him with a plate of poisonous mushrooms at a banquet. Although Claudius was 63 years old at the time, and not in the best of health, his death so soon after Nero had been declared heir and was best placed to inherit seems too fortuitous to have been a mere coincidence, particularly considering Agrippina's previous conduct.

Some historians have speculated that Nero himself may have even played a role in Claudius's death. Suetonius wrote of Nero, "[E]ven if he was not the instigator of the emperor's death, he was at least privy to it, as he openly admitted; for he used afterwards to laud mushrooms, the vehicle in which the poison was administered to Claudius, as 'the food of the gods,' as the Greek proverb has it. At any rate, after Claudius's death he vented on him every kind of insult, in act and word, charging him now with folly and now with cruelty; for it was a favourite joke of his to say that Claudius had ceased 'to play the fool among mortals,' lengthening the first syllable of the word morari, and he disregarded many of his decrees and acts as the work of a madman and a dotard. Finally, he neglected to enclose the place where his body was burned except with a low and mean wall."

Whether Claudius's death was natural or the result of foul play, however, one thing was clear. There was only one person who could inherit, and that was the 17 year old Nero, his heir.

## Chapter 2: Nero Consolidates Power, 54-63 A.D.

### Early Reign

**Coin of Nero and Poppaea Sabina**

At 17, Nero was the youngest to ever become a Roman emperor, and not surprisingly the teen was still highly malleable. Though he was slyer than his predecessor Claudius, who by all accounts had let Agrippina wrap him around her finger, he was still a teenaged boy who had been raised in pampered seclusion, and he was extremely susceptible both to the will of his mother, of whom he held in awe. He was also heavily shaped by the teachings of his tutor, Seneca, and his newfound friend the Praetorian general Sextus Burrus. Perhaps recognizing his own naivete and limitations, upon taking power in 54 A.D., Nero promised the Senate more autonomy.

Naturally, the most influential people who had Nero's ear had different motives and goals, inevitably leading to rivalries among them. Agrippina, who had been named a priestess of the cult of the deified Claudius, was granted an unprecedented level of power and privilege by actually being allowed to listen in, from behind a curtain, to Senate meetings and other official matters of state. For a woman, this was utterly unheard of, and Seneca and Burrus were both jealous and wary of her newfound powers and sought to curb them at every turn. They recognized Agrippina as an immoral, power-hungry degenerate, and wisely reasoned that the less power she effectively wielded, the better.

Cracks were already beginning to show during the first year of Nero's reign, when in a moment of uncharacteristic diplomatic zeal (it appears as though Nero spent more time in brothels than in the Senate in 54 A.D.), he met an Armenian diplomatic mission. Seneca narrowly avoided a catastrophe by preventing her from casually sitting down alongside her son, something which would have been an extremely grave breach of diplomatic protocol. It was unheard of for a woman to even be in the room while the men discussed diplomacy, and just the latest example that Agrippina was overstepping her bounds.

The following year, Nero sat as consul for the first time and began to enact some remarkably enlightened populist policies, including the prosecution of many corrupt officials and the lowering of tax rates he considered extortionate. Around the same time, he also became involved with Claudia Acte, a freedwoman, despite his marriage to Octavia. The affair was highly public and an embarrassment to his wife, and Agrippina was determined to put a stop to it. Revelling in his new-found power and popularity, however, and supported by Seneca, Nero balked. This led to an estrangement that would never be reconciled.

55 A.D. was also the year that Nero began casting off his chains. Agrippina was virtually banned from public affairs, while Seneca, Burrus and Marcus Antonius Pallas, the freedman who had convinced Claudius to marry Agrippina, were accused of a number of crimes ranging from embezzlement to having relations with Agrippina. Seneca succeeded in having all three of them acquitted, though Pallas lost his position, but they received such a scare that they were disinclined to re-enter into public affairs and were content to act unofficially as Nero's advisers.

Agrippina, furious at Nero's deliberate challenge to what she perceived as her rightful authority, began to cultivate his older half-brother Britannicus, whom she appears to have wanted to set upon the throne in his place, hoping he would be more biddable. Britannicus had the better claim, and with Agrippina's backing he posed a genuine threat to Nero's recently acquired crown, so it seems he acted late in 55 A.D. Britannicus, who was a young teenager and in full health, suddenly and mysteriously died after falling ill at a banquet. Foul play was almost certainly involved, with the ancient sources suggesting that Britannicus was poisoned by Nero by having the poison added to the water Romans used to reduce the potency of their extremely powerful wines. The wine would have been tasted, but the water would not, and so an inconvenient threat to Nero's rule was conveniently removed. Ancient historians claimed Nero hired Locusta, a woman who specialized in poisons, and that when her first test poison failed to kill a slave, Nero threatened to have her put to death. Locusta then came up with the new poison used on Britannicus, which she allegedly promised would "kill swifter than a viper."

Over the following three years, Nero's rule proved neither better nor worse than that of any other Emperor. Nero had his vices, but that had been true of Claudius and Caligula as well (if less so for the iron-willed Tiberius and Octavian), and vice was never a barrier to public affection. After all, Mark Antony had been a hero of the people and the army, despite being an inveterate gambler and lecher. Thus, Nero continued to be popular with the common people, especially the lower classes, even though some of his policies incited a strong backlash. One of these was the ratification of a law proposed by the Senate permitting the execution of a slave's entire family if they committed a crime. Despite rioting in Rome over the matter, and the fact he had earlier vetoed a Senatorial law that would allow freedmen to revert to slave status for specific crimes, Nero allowed the law to be passed, a bizarre about-face in policy that shows he was perhaps beginning to become erratic.

In 58 B.C., Nero first began an affair with Poppaea, the wife of one of his closest friends, the future emperor Otho. Though this is sometimes described as a catalyst for his notorious matricide the following year, such a link seems unlikely. The estrangement had begun well before, when Nero had first forced his mother from public affairs and she had turned, in disgust, to Britannicus as a more biddable puppet. However, his mother also disapproved of Nero's relationship with Poppaea, as she had of his previous one with Claudia. Agrippina's disapproval is hard to understand, given her own adulterous proclivities, but perhaps hypocrisy was another of her long list of vices. Either way, it definitely put an even further strain on their relationship.

**Matricide**

Whether it was due to this new cause or simply a build up of all of them, in 59 B.C. the strain in Nero's relationship with his mother reached its breaking point. That year, Nero decided to commit his most notorious and greatest crime so far: matricide.

Accounts of how the murder was carried out differ substantially, sometimes contradicting one another, but certain common details emerge. It appears likely that, having decided that having Agrippina assassinated would incite too much suspicion, Nero devised a plan to make her death look like an accident. Ancient historians wrote that Nero had a wooden boat constructed with a collapsible lead ceiling, the idea being that when the mechanism was put into action, the ceiling would fall and either kill Agrippina outright or cause the boat to sink, thus drowning her. On her next sea voyage, Agrippina boarded Nero's death-ship. The lead ceiling, however, supposedly failed to work, either because Agrippina took refuge under a couch as it collapsed or because it did not succeed in sinking the boat, and the boat was scuppered either by its own crew or by another ship that was notionally riding escort. Agrippina, however, survived the boat's sinking and succeeded in swimming ashore, having realised that the men on the other boat were also commanded to kill her. According to Tacitus, Agrippina's friend Acerronia made for the escort ship instead of swimming to shore, calling out that she was Agrippina in an effort to encourage them to rescue her even more quickly. Clearly unaware of the plot, Acerronia had inadvertently hastened her own death, and in an ironic twist she was bludgeoned to death by the ship's oarsmen who mistook her for Agrippina.

Though she survived Nero's death-ship, Agrippina did not live for long. When he learned that she was still alive, and likely to start making embarrassing speeches, Nero quickly dispatched three assassins to murder her. Reportedly, when the assassins arrived, Agrippina told them to strike at her womb first.

**The Remorse of the Emperor Nero after the Murder of his Mother, by John William
Waterhouse, 1878.**

Nero was supposedly beside himself at her funeral, though whether with grief or relief it is
hard to tell. His friends and advisers lavished him with praise for having finally rid himself of the
constant threat his mother posed, but other threats would quickly rear themselves on the horizon,
and not just against his person, but against Rome itself.

### Foreign Threats

In 60 A.D., while the governor of Britannia, Gaius Paulinus, was besieging the island of
Anglesey, the southern tribes of Britain rebelled. Led by Boudicca of the Iceni, the tribes burned
three major cities, including Londonium, putting the fate of Roman Britannia severely at risk.
Paulinus, however, was able to crush the uprising, and Boudicca killed herself rather than be
taken prisoner. Nero, showing his customary gratitude, removed Paulinus from office after his
victory out of fear that he was becoming too powerful.

Britannia was safe, but another part of the Empire quickly became endangered. This time, it
was the client state of Armenia whose fate was in the balance. In 62 A.D., hostilities once again
flared up with Rome's age-old enemy, Parthia. Although Gnaeus Corbulo had suppressed a
Parthian invasion on Nero's orders, war quickly escalated once more in 58 A.D., this time
because Tigranes, the puppet-king installed by Nero in Armenia, invaded Parthian territory.
Border hostilities quickly looked likely to escalate into all-out war, but Nero skillfully defused
the situation by ignoring his more jingoistic commanders and negotiating a peace deal, knowing
budget issues were a serious concern. Nero succeeded in convincing the former, Parthian-
installed king of Armenia, Tiridates, to come to Rome and accept his crown from Nero's own
hands in 63 A.D., in a ceremony meant to show his subservience to Rome. This caused Nero's
stock to rise significantly, especially in the East, since he had avoided Rome a costly war.

## Pisonian Conspiracy

62 A.D. was a difficult year for Nero, not just because of the escalating Parthian crisis. Burrus, one of his most trusted advisors, died of disease that year, and Seneca was once more accused of embezzlement and forced to retire. Nero also finally divorced Octavia, putting an end to his (by all accounts) extremely unhappy marriage. In her place Nero married Poppaea, who was both carrying his child and divorced from Otho.

Additionally, the Senate began to worry that Nero, who had made extravagant promises of giving them more power than during the Republican era, was actually engaged in subverting all of their power. Conspiracies began to spring up, and Nero put to death a number of important figures for treason between 62 and 63, including Marcus Antonius Pallas. Many were put to death without any particular rhyme or reason, or even public indictment. With most of the moderating influences – for bad or good – gone from his life, Nero was fast degenerating from absolute ruler to all-out tyrant.

## Chapter 3: A World on Fire

**Agrippina crowning Nero Emperor.**

### The Great Fire

On the night of July 18th, 64 A.D., the most significant event of Nero's time in power – and the one which, for better or for worse, would seal his name in infamy throughout the ages – took place. What became known as the Great Fire of Rome erupted sometime between the night of the 18th and the earliest hours of the 19th, and it consumed almost a quarter of the city while it burned out of control for five days. Interestingly, though there is archaeological evidence for the fact that the fire actually took place, and its extent was as significant as the sources seem to indicate, Tacitus is the only one who gives a comprehensive account of the fire, with other biographers not even mentioning it (aside from Pliny, who mentions it in connection to another incident). Yet the fire was definitely a momentous event, and one which would live on in history as Nero's worst hour.

Despite popular belief, it is extremely unlikely that Nero caused the fire. Though legend – and some ancient historians – claim that Nero wanted to create space for the palace he eventually erected over much of the ruins, the fabled *Domus Aurea* (Golden Mansion) there are several facts that contradict this theory. First, Tacitus, who was actually alive at the time of Nero's reign, suggests that he was not in Rome at all, but in nearby Antium. Secondly, astronomers have established that the night of July 18th/July 19th was two days shy of a full moon, which seems to make arson unlikely – after all, incendiarists would hardly want to pick a night during which they would be most likely to be seen to perpetrate a crime. Moreover, the fire itself actually damaged a significant part of the *Domus Transitoria*, Nero's palace prior to the *Domus Aurea*, and though the fire that he planned may have gotten out of control, it is unlikely that he would have wanted – or even risked – setting his own home alight.

Suetonius and Cassius Dio, two of Nero's ancient biographers, are adamant that it was he himself who set the fire (or ordered it set), and they are the originators of the myth that Nero played the lyre, dancing around his palace and singing "The Sack of Troy" while Rome burned outside his windows. The popular canard that Nero "fiddled while Rome burned" still remains well known nearly 2,000 years after the fire, even though no fiddle existed in 1st century Rome. For his part, Tacitus vehemently denied those accounts, calling such a story apocryphal and untrue.

Of course, Christians were probably no more likely to blame than Nero. What appears most likely is that the fire was an accident, likely caused by flammable materials near the Circus Maximus. Indeed, blazes of such kind were common until the 19th century, in overcrowded cities with wooden houses closely packed together, lit and heated by open flames and with no organized official fire brigades. Rome would suffer two more major fires in the next 15 years.

Whatever its origin, the fire was a disaster for Rome. Though casualties are unknown, it destroyed scores, if not hundreds, of private residences, commercial premises, and public buildings. According to Tacitus, Nero quickly hurried back from Antium when news reached him of the fire, and opened the doors of his palace to common people dispossessed by the flames. Tacitus claim Nero also spent days, sometimes without his bodyguards, combing the smoking ruins for victims and partially funding the relief effort out of his own private fortune. Though this is partially at odds with Nero's perceived character, his populist generosity to the lower classes, which is a hallmark of his reign, is in keeping with his previous legislation and sounds like it could have a kernel of truth.

The aftermath of the fire must have been a sight to behold. Much of Rome was a scorched and smoking ruin, and Nero was now faced with the unenviable task of trying to finance a rebuilding effort with state coffers that were already dangerously close to being empty. Part of his economic policy included the transportation of rubble from the blaze to nearby Ostia, where it was poured into the marshes both to get rid of it and to drain them of water, creating what eventually would become fertile farmland. Nero also ordered the reconstruction of the areas affected by the fire, having modern, evenly spaced and comfortable residences erected under his own supervision, and presumably employing many of those whose livelihoods were destroyed by the flames.

In typical Nero fashion, however, he also looked to his own private gain, and much of the land that had been cleared by the fire was converted into his sprawling *Domus Aurea,* a massive palatial complex which extended between 100 and 300 acres and also included a 30-metre colossus of Nero himself. The *Domus Aurea* may very well have been a building project that cost more than the remaining reconstruction effort on its own. In order to finance all of this, Nero was forced to devalue the Roman currency, an event which had never occurred in the history of the Roman Empire. The silver denarius and the gold aureus were both reduced in weight, and the purity of the precious metals they contained also dropped by a significant amount. The extravagance of the *Domus Aurea,* coupled with the devaluation of the currency and the natural outrage felt by many Romans in the wake of the fire (arson was still believed to be the cause of the blaze) meant that Nero quickly began to incur a significant backlash. For almost the first time, the people were against him. He needed a scapegoat.

Conveniently, there was the perfect one at hand: Christians. The secretive sect, which still boasted only small numbers but was fast growing in popularity, was viewed with suspicion and even hatred, as the Jews also were, by much of the Roman Empire. The main reason for this dislike was simple: the other pagan polytheistic traditions which flourished side by side throughout the Empire might advocate the superiority of their own particular Gods but, unlike the Christians, would not deny the existence of others. Christians flat-out believed that theirs was the only true God, and were not afraid to say so. Consequently, they were highly unpopular.

Nero capitalised on that unpopularity by accusing Christians of being responsible for the blaze, though it does not appear as though any motive was ever ascribed to them. Several were seized and, after being tortured, confessed (it is unclear whether they confessed to being Christians, or to the arson itself, but most sources are in accord in saying that they confessed *because* they were tortured). Scores of Christians were martyred, some draped in the skins of wild animals and then torn apart by dogs in the arena, others crucified in a mockery of Jesus's martyrdom, and still more were burned alive, nightly, to serve as illumination for Nero's garden banquets. The first institutionalised persecution of the Christians in the history of the Roman Empire (but not the last) had begun.

Tacitus described Nero's scapegoating of the Christians, writing, "Consequently, to get rid of the report, Nero fastened the guilt and inflicted the most exquisite tortures on a class hated for their abominations, called Christians by the populace. Christus, from whom the name had its origin, suffered the extreme penalty during the reign of Tiberius at the hands of one of our procurators, Pontius Pilatus, and a most mischievous superstition, thus checked for the moment, again broke out not only in Judaea, the first source of the evil, but even in Rome, where all things hideous and shameful from every part of the world find their centre and become popular. Accordingly, an arrest was first made of all who pleaded guilty; then, upon their information, an immense multitude was convicted, not so much of the crime of firing the city, as of hatred against mankind. Mockery of all sorts was added to their deaths. Covered with the skins of beasts, they were torn by dogs and perished, or were nailed to crosses, or were doomed to the flames and burnt, to serve as a nightly illumination, when daylight had expired."

## The Pisonian Conspiracy

**Nero coin, circa 66. Ara Pacis on the reverse.**

Blaming the Christians afforded Nero some momentary respite, but other problems swiftly came to the fore. Nero began, increasingly, to lose control. He had always had an appetite for popular adulation – hence his populist legislation – but that appetite now escalated into all-out mania. A fan of poetry, theatre and other performing arts, Nero had initially kept his performances (which by all accounts were quite terrible) confined to a small circle of hangers-on and subordinates, but between 64 A.D. and 65 A.D. he decided that it was time to win more support for himself among the population. Nero apparently thought he could do so by performing publicly.

Though there is evidence that he was encouraged both by his inner circle and members of the Senate to perform as a means of boosting his support among the lower classes, it seems unlikely that these performances were well-received. While the Greeks might hold theatre sacred, generally in Rome it was a far less refined art, more akin to pantomime, and actors and actresses had a reputation for being promiscuous and immoral, just a step above prostitutes. For the Emperor – who was also the *Pontifex Maximus*, one of the main religious figures – to engage in such a degrading activity was unheard of among the Romans.

Most of his ancient biographers are disdainful of Nero's theatrical endeavours, and it appears as though they were one of the major catalysts for the Pisonian conspiracy, a plot orchestrated in 65 A.D. by Gaius Calpurnius Piso (who had been working against Nero since 63 A.D. at least) with the complicity of two Praetorian officers, Sulpicius Asper and Subrius Flavius. The plot, which had Republican ambitions, failed because it was discovered by one of Nero's freedmen, and eventually reported to his secretary. Piso, Asper and Flavius were publicly executed along with a number of other people also implicated in the plot. Ironically, one of these was the poet and historiographer Lucan, who wrote an epic poem about Caesar's victory over Pompey the Great at the Battle of Pharsalus and was one of the kindest sources for Nero's reign, praising his economic policies and the prosperity the Empire experienced under his rule. It's possible that Lucan's pro-Republican writings later in his life gave Nero cause to have him executed. Another notable victim of the Pisonian conspiracy was Nero's old tutor Seneca, who had apparently been informed of the plot but failed to report it. Seneca was commanded to kill himself by Nero, which he duly did.

**Bust of Lucan**

65 A.D. also marked the year in which Nero's wife Poppaea, possibly the last restraining influence in his life, died. It is unclear whether Poppaea died in childbirth, or whether, as Suetonius suggests, Nero kicked her to death, but whatever the case, he seems not to have felt much grief.

**Chapter 4: Nero's Final Years**

The following year, in 66 A.D., Nero married Statilia Messalina, and then in 67 A.D. he scandalized much of Roman society by taking to "wife" in a formal ceremony one of his freedmen, a young boy named Sporus, whom Nero had castrated. Sporus, who was said to resemble Poppaea, appeared next to Nero in official ceremonies dressed as a woman and was treated in many ways like Nero's wife. This went to add itself to the long list of Nero's supposed depravities, including another homosexual marriage, incest with his mother, and the alleged rape of a vestal virgin. Popular opinion for Nero was now at an all-time low.

Nero was given no respite. In 66 A.D., revolt broke out in the ever-unquiet province of Judaea and quickly escalated into all-out war. To contain the crisis, Nero sent the future emperor Vespasian to pacify the region in 67 A.D. Nero, never the battlefield commander, did not attend the campaign, as he was otherwise employed. Specifically, he was in Greece, participating in the Olympics. This had apparently been suggested by Nero's advisers, who reckoned having him do so would strengthen the ties between Rome and Greece (then a province), though in the event his attendance was a disaster. Participating in one of the chariot races, Nero was thrown from the chariot during a particularly curve and almost died, an event which seems to have made him subsequently lose his nerve, since he dropped out of at least another race. However, he was crowned with the winner's laurels all the same, either because the Greeks did not want to offend Nero, or because, as some uncharitable biographers have suggested, he bribed the judges to give him the crown. The revolt in Judaea, meanwhile, continued to give Vespasian problems, but Nero was oblivious. What he did not realise was that, at last, the cracks were beginning to show. The Romans were finally beginning to tire of Nero's extravagance, and the stage was being set for the finale of his life's tragedy.

# Vespasian

In 68 A.D., matters finally came to a head for Nero. Gaius Vindex, the governor of one of the provinces of Gaul (territory surrounding modern Lyon), rebelled. Vindex, who reportedly felt that Nero's taxation of the Western provinces was exceedingly unfair, had a strong force at his back, but knew he could not face Rome's wrath alone. Accordingly, he sent out messages to Servius Galba, the governor of one of the adjoining provinces (Pyrenean Spain), begging him to join in the rebellion and pledging his support if Galba would declare himself emperor in defiance of Nero. Galba, however, wavered, though he did not denounce Vindex as a traitor, as he might have done.

Without the support of Galba, this allowed Lucius Rufus, the general sent by a panicked Nero to crush the rebellion with extreme prejudice, to engage Vindex in battle at Vesontio, where Vindex's force was crushed. Rather than allow himself to be taken prisoner, Vindex committed suicide, in the traditional manner of the Roman aristocracy, but then, in an act that surprised even their own commander, Verginius's legionaries attempted to mutiny and proclaim him Emperor. Verginius refused to rebel, but Galba was now openly defying Nero's commands, and Nero's woes were compounded when the Praetorian general, Gaius Sabinus, mutinied and went over to Galba. This was a colossal development, as the Praetorian Guard was the Emperor's own personal legionary force and literally his extended bodyguard. Having them abandon him was catastrophic.

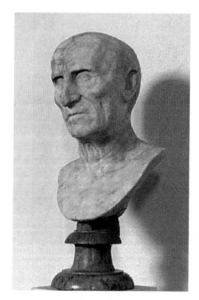

# Galba

Having lost the loyalty of the Praetorian Guard, Nero panicked. Terrified of what the Praetorians might do to him if they got their hands on him, he fled the *Domus Aurea* in secret. Nero intended to make for Ostia and board a ship for the Eastern provinces, where his stock was still significantly higher than in the West ever since his deal with Parthia. However, army officers who sensed the way the wind was blowing flatly refused to obey his orders, leaving him without an escort.

At a loss, Nero found himself despairing, quickly reviewing and discarding a variety of plans. Nero considered fleeing all the way to Parthia, throwing himself on the mercy of the Parthian rulers and living out his life as a pretender prince in exile. Nero may have also contemplated appealing to Galba himself to let him live, a highly risky proposition since Galba would almost certainly have Nero quietly dispatched once he was in power. Nero even considered giving a public speech renouncing his power and begging the people to pardon him, or, if that was too much to ask, to let him retire to Egypt as a prefect. Nero must have gauged the temper of the people as too angry, however, or realized that it was highly unlikely he would be allowed to retire in golden exile. Whatever Nero was thinking, he ultimately decided to head back to the *Domus Aurea,* where apparently he fell into a restless sleep.

In the middle of the night, Nero is said to have awakened and discovered that his personal bodyguard had fled the palace. He quickly sent messages via his few remaining slaves to his closest associates and assorted hangers-on, only to discover that these fair-weather friends had also sensed that something was amiss and hastily made themselves scarce. Nero then screamed for anyone who had any skill with a blade to kill him, terrified of what might happen if he were taken alive, but no one was prepared to oblige. Nero reportedly fled wailing from the *Domus Aurea*, determined to hurl himself into the Tiber but quickly reconsidered, and after that fit of madness had passed he returned to the palace. One of his freedmen, displaying remarkable loyalty, offered to shelter Nero in his villa, several miles outside of the city walls. Desperate enough to clutch at any straw, Nero agreed, and disguised himself before once again fleeing the *Domus Aurea* with four of his most trusted servants, including his Greek secretary Epaphroditos (who had first brought him news of the Pisonian conspiracy three years earlier) and Sporus, his castrated lover.

Once at the freedman's villa, Nero seems to have regained a measure of composure and resigned himself to death, or possibly he was still indulging his penchant for histrionics, even at the eleventh hour. He ordered his servants to dig a grave for him, but his composure was interrupted by a messenger who brought him the disquieting news that the Senate had declared him an Enemy of Rome and had given orders for his execution by the charming method of having him beaten to death with sticks. This caused Nero, never the bravest of men, to panic once again, and he determined to have done with it and kill himself in the traditional Roman manner by opening his own stomach with his sword.

Fittingly, Nero seems to have been incapable of even dying properly. Preparing to kill himself, Nero first asked one of his companions to lead the way by committing suicide himself and showing how it was done. But with his fear overcoming his resolve, he began to weep and eventually ordered Epaphroditos to do the deed. Initially reluctant, Epaphroditos finally half-heartedly stabbed Nero in the gut, an act which later induced Domitian to execute Epaphroditos himself for failing to prevent Nero's suicide. As Nero lay dying of blood-loss on the couch, one of the riders dispatched by the Senate to arrest him burst into the villa and, seeing him, attempted to staunch his wounds in vain. Nero perished shortly thereafter. It was June 9th, 68 A.D., the anniversary of the death of his first wife, Claudia Octavia.

**Marble bust of Nero, Antiquarium of the Palatine.**

### Chapter 5: The Aftermath of Nero's Death and Nero's Legacy

News of Nero's death was apparently greeted by cheering in the streets of Rome, though reports are contradictory. The aristocracy and ruling classes were definitely relieved to be rid of him, though had they known what was in store they might have changed their minds. Nero's death also spelled the end of the Julio-Claudian line that had dated back to Augustus, and with that line extinguished, there was no accepted heir to the throne. What followed was the chaotic Year of the Four Emperors, a viciously cut-throat internecine war in which Galba first took power, followed by Otho, closely followed by Vitellius and then finally by Vespasian, who succeeded at last in restoring order.

Interestingly, Nero seems to have developed something of an Arthurian legend following his death. Like the Once and Future King, Nero was supposed to one day return, though in this case his return was not meant to be a positive matter. Many people also refused to believe, for some reason, that Nero (who was buried without ceremony in his family vault) was actually dead. In the turbulent years following his death, many impostors pretended to be Nero (or more rarely, his son), and they cropped up all across the Roman Empire. These impostors were usually quickly dealt with or, once they attracted too much official attention, dispatched by their own followers, but they are a testimony to Nero's remarkable staying power as a notorious figure. Dio Chrysostom, a contemporary Greek historian, claimed that the impostors popped up because Nero was actually still popular among the lower classes. "Indeed the truth about this has not come out even yet; for so far as the rest of his subjects were concerned, there was nothing to prevent his continuing to be Emperor for all time, seeing that even now everybody wishes he were still alive. And the great majority do believe that he still is, although in a certain sense he has died not once but often along with those who had been firmly convinced that he was still alive."

Without question, in the aftermath of Nero's death, it was apparent even among contemporaries that some of the contradicting stories and appraisals of his life and tyranny were fanciful and false. As the ancient historian Josephus explained, "But I omit any further discourse about these affairs; for there have been a great many who have composed the history of Nero; some of which have departed from the truth of facts out of favor, as having received benefits from him; while others, out of hatred to him, and the great ill-will which they bore him, have so impudently raved against him with their lies, that they justly deserve to be condemned. Nor do I wonder at such as have told lies of Nero, since they have not in their writings preserved the truth of history as to those facts that were earlier than his time, even when the actors could have no way incurred their hatred, since those writers lived a long time after them."

Regardless, however, Nero is not exactly a polarizing figure. Despite the bias that many of his biographers (particularly the Christian ones) might have felt against him, it is hard to deny the fact that for every good thing he might have done – helped with the Great Fire relief effort, promoted enlightened populist laws – he committed two despicable acts. Though modern historians can discard the wilder rumours about his life, such as his incest with Agrippina, or his responsibility in starting the Great Fire of Rome, what remains still paints the portrait of a thoroughly vile individual. Nero was a vain, arrogant, cowardly, weak-willed human being who almost certainly murdered his own mother, treated his various wives like dirt (and possibly killed one of them), and arranged the murder of his half-brother. Additionally, he was also a sadist who actively enjoyed inflicting pain, or watching it inflicted. When he decided to blame the Christians for the blaze of 64 A.D., no matter how reviled they might be, he could have dispatched the alleged culprits quickly. Instead, he chose to torture them to death, making them die unimaginably horrific deaths. His legacy is a few scattered ruins, the most important of which – the *Domus Aurea* – he built for his own personal enjoyment, and a reputation as black as any in history.

According to ancient accounts, one unnamed Roman, upon seeing Nero with Sporus, is said to have remarked that it would have been better if Gnaeus had also consorted with such an individual instead of impregnating Agrippina. Sadly, that might have been the most apt analysis of Nero's life and reign. Perhaps it would have been better for everyone involved if he had never been born at all.

## Suetonius's Life of Nero

I. Two celebrated families, the Calvini and Aenobarbi, sprung from the race of the Domitii. The Aenobarbi derive both their extraction and their cognomen from one Lucius Domitius, of whom we have this tradition: --As he was returning out of the country to Rome, he was met by two young men of a most august appearance, who desired him to announce to the senate and people a victory, of which no certain intelligence had yet reached the city. To prove that they were more than mortals, they stroked his cheeks, and thus changed his hair, which was black, to a bright colour, resembling that of brass; which mark of distinction descended to his posterity, for they had generally red beards. This family had the honour of seven consulships, one triumph, and two censorships; and being admitted into the patrician order, they continued the use of the same cognomen, with no other praenomina than those of Cneius and Lucius. These, however, they assumed with singular irregularity; three persons in succession sometimes adhering to one of them, and then they were changed alternately. For the first, second, and third of the Aenobarbi had the praenomen of Lucius, and again the three following, successively, that of Cneius, while those who came after were called, by turns, one, Lucius, and the other, Cneius. It appears to me proper to give a short account of several of the family, to show that Nero so far degenerated from the noble qualities of his ancestors, that he retained only their vices; as if those alone had been transmitted to him by his descent.

II. To begin, therefore, at a remote period, his great-grandfather's grandfather, Cneius Domitius, when he was tribune of the people, being offended with the high priests for electing another than himself in the room of his father, obtained the transfer of the right of election from the colleges of the priests to the people. In his consulship, having conquered the Allobroges and the Arverni, he made a progress through the province, mounted upon an elephant, with a body of soldiers attending him, in a sort of triumphal pomp. Of this person the orator Licinius Crassus said, "It was no wonder he had a brazen beard, who had a face of iron, and a heart of lead." His son, during his praetorship, proposed that Cneius Caesar, upon the expiration of his consulship, should be called to account before the senate for his administration of that office, which was supposed to be contrary both to the omens and the laws. Afterwards, when he was consul himself, he tried to deprive Cneius of the command of the army, and having been, by intrigue and cabal, appointed his successor, he was made prisoner at Corsinium, in the beginning of the civil war. Being set at liberty, he went to Marseilles, which was then besieged; where having, by his presence, animated the people to hold out, he suddenly deserted them, and at last was slain in the battle of Pharsalia. He was a man of little constancy, and of a sullen temper. In despair of his fortunes, he had recourse to poison, but was so terrified at the thoughts of death, that, immediately repenting, he took a vomit to throw it up again, and gave freedom to his physician for having, with great prudence and wisdom, given him only a gentle dose of the poison. When Cneius Pompey was consulting with his friends in what manner he should conduct himself towards those who were neuter and took no part in the contest, he was the only one who proposed that they should be treated as enemies.

III. He left a son, who was, without doubt, the best of the family. By the Pedian law, he was condemned, although innocent, amongst others who were concerned in the death of Caesar. Upon this, he went over to Brutus and Cassius, his near relations; and, after their death, not only kept together the fleet, the command of which had been given him some time before, but even increased it. At last, when the party had everywhere been defeated, he voluntarily surrendered it to Mark Antony; considering it as a piece of service for which the latter owed him no small obligations. Of all those who were condemned by the law above-mentioned, he was the only man who was restored to his country, and filled the highest offices. When the civil war again broke out, he was appointed lieutenant under the same Antony, and offered the chief command by those who were ashamed of Cleopatra; but not daring, on account of a sudden indisposition with which he was seized, either to accept or refuse it, he went over to Augustus, and died a few days after, not without an aspersion cast upon his memory. For Antony gave out, that he was induced to change sides by his impatience to be with his mistress, Servilia Nais.

IV. This Cneius had a son, named Domitius, who was afterwards well known as the nominal purchaser of the family property left by Augustus's will; and no less famous in his youth for his dexterity in chariot-driving, than he was afterwards for the triumphal ornaments which he obtained in the German war. But he was a man of great arrogance, prodigality, and cruelty. When he was aedile, he obliged Lucius Plancus, the censor, to give him the way; and in his praetorship, and consulship, he made Roman knights and married women act on the stage. He gave hunts of wild beasts, both in the Circus and in all the wards of the city; as also a show of gladiators; but with such barbarity, that Augustus, after privately reprimanding him, to no purpose, was obliged to restrain him by a public edict.

V. By the elder Antonia he had Nero's father, a man of execrable character in every part of his life. During his attendance upon Caius Caesar in the East, he killed a freedman of his own, for refusing to drink as much as he ordered him. Being dismissed for this from Caesar's society, he did not mend his habits; for, in a village upon the Appian road, he suddenly whipped his horses, and drove his chariot, on purpose, over a poor boy, crushing him to pieces. At Rome, he struck out the eye of a Roman knight in the Forum, only for some free language in a dispute between them. He was likewise so fraudulent, that he not only cheated some silversmiths of the price of goods he had bought of them, but, during his praetorship, defrauded the owners of chariots in the Circensian games of the prizes due to them for their victory. His sister, jeering him for the complaints made by the leaders of the several parties, he agreed to sanction a law, "That, for the future, the prizes should be immediately paid." A little before the death of Tiberius, he was prosecuted for treason, adulteries, and incest with his sister Lepida, but escaped in the timely change of affairs, and died of a dropsy, at Pyrgi; leaving behind him his son, Nero, whom he had by Agrippina, the daughter of Germanicus.

VI. Nero was born at Antium, nine months after the death of Tiberius, upon the eighteenth of the calends of January [15th December], just as the sun rose, so that its beams touched him before they could well reach the earth. While many fearful conjectures, in respect to his future fortune, were formed by different persons, from the circumstances of his nativity, a saying of his father, Domitius, was regarded as an ill presage, who told his friends who were congratulating him upon the occasion, "That nothing but what was detestable, and pernicious to the public, could ever be produced of him and Agrippina." Another manifest prognostic of his future infelicity occurred upon his lustration day. For Caius Caesar being requested by his sister to give the child what name he thought proper--looking at his uncle, Claudius, who afterwards, when emperor, adopted Nero, he gave his: and this not seriously, but only in jest; Agrippina treating it with contempt, because Claudius at that time was a mere laughing-stock at the palace. He lost his father when he was three years old, being left heir to a third part of his estate; of which he never got possession, the whole being seized by his co-heir, Caius. His mother being soon after banished, he lived with his aunt Lepida, in a very necessitous condition, under the care of two tutors, a dancing-master and a barber. After Claudius came to the empire, he not only recovered his father's estate, but was enriched with the additional inheritance of that of his step-father, Crispus Passienus. Upon his mother's recall from banishment, he was advanced to such favour, through Nero's powerful interest with the emperor, that it was reported, assassins were employed by Messalina, Claudius's wife, to strangle him, as Britannicus's rival, whilst he was taking his noon-day repose. In addition to the story, it was said that they were frightened by a serpent, which crept from under his cushion, and ran away. The tale was occasioned by finding on his couch, near the pillow, the skin of a snake, which, by his mother's order, he wore for some time upon his right arm, inclosed in a bracelet of gold. This amulet, at last, he laid aside, from aversion to her memory; but he sought for it again, in vain, in the time of his extremity.

VII. When he was yet a mere boy, before he arrived at the age of puberty, during the celebration of the Circensian games, he performed his part in the Trojan play with a degree of firmness which gained him great applause. In the eleventh year of his age, he was adopted by Claudius, and placed under the tuition of Annaeus Seneca, who had been made a senator. It is said, that Seneca dreamt the night after, that he was giving a lesson to Caius Caesar. Nero soon verified his dream, betraying the cruelty of his disposition in every way he could. For he attempted to persuade his father that his brother, Britannicus, was nothing but a changeling, because the latter had saluted him, notwithstanding his adoption, by the name of Aenobarbus, as usual. When his aunt, Lepida, was brought to trial, he appeared in court as a witness against her, to gratify his mother, who persecuted the accused. On his introduction into the Forum, at the age of manhood, he gave a largess to the people and a donative to the soldiers: for the pretorian cohorts, he appointed a solemn procession under arms, and marched at the head of them with a shield in his hand; after which he went to return thanks to his father in the senate. Before Claudius, likewise, at the time he was consul, he made a speech for the Bolognese, in Latin, and for the Rhodians and people of Ilium, in Greek. He had the jurisdiction of praefect of the city, for the first time, during the Latin festival; during which the most celebrated advocates brought before him, not short and trifling causes, as is usual in that case, but trials of importance, notwithstanding they had instructions from Claudius himself to the contrary. Soon afterwards, he married Octavia, and exhibited the Circensian games, and hunting of wild beasts, in honour of Claudius.

VIII. He was seventeen years of age at the death of that prince, and as soon as that event was made public, he went out to the cohort on guard between the hours of six and seven; for the omens were so disastrous, that no earlier time of the day was judged proper. On the steps before the palace gate, he was unanimously saluted by the soldiers as their emperor, and then carried in a litter to the camp; thence, after making a short speech to the troops, into the senate-house, where he continued until the evening; of all the immense honours which were heaped upon him, refusing none but the title of Father of his country, on account of his youth,

IX. He began his reign with an ostentation of dutiful regard to the memory of Claudius, whom he buried with the utmost pomp and magnificence, pronouncing the funeral oration himself, and then had him enrolled amongst the gods. He paid likewise the highest honours to the memory of his father Domitius. He left the management of affairs, both public and private, to his mother. The word which he gave the first day of his reign to the tribune on guard, was, "The Best of Mothers," and afterwards he frequently appeared with her in the streets of Rome in her litter. He settled a colony at Antium, in which he placed the veteran soldiers belonging to the guards; and obliged several of the richest centurions of the first rank to transfer their residence to that place; where he likewise made a noble harbour at a prodigious expense.

X. To establish still further his character, he declared, "that he designed to govern according to the model of Augustus;" and omitted no opportunity of showing his generosity, clemency, and complaisance. The more burthensome taxes he either entirely took off, or diminished. The rewards appointed for informers by the Papian law, he reduced to a fourth part, and distributed to the people four hundred sesterces a man. To the noblest of the senators who were much reduced in their circumstances, he granted annual allowances, in some cases as much as five hundred thousand sesterces; and to the pretorian cohorts a monthly allowance of corn gratis. When called upon to subscribe the sentence, according to custom, of a criminal condemned to die, "I wish," said he, "I had never learnt to read and write." He continually saluted people of the several orders by name, without a prompter. When the senate returned him their thanks for his good government, he replied to them, "It will be time enough to do so when I shall have deserved it." He admitted the common people to see him perform his exercises in the Campus Martius. He frequently declaimed in public, and recited verses of his own composing, not only at home, but in the theatre; so much to the joy of all the people, that public prayers were appointed to be put up to the gods upon that account; and the verses which had been publicly read, were, after being written in gold letters, consecrated to Jupiter Capitolinus.

XI. He presented the people with a great number and variety of spectacles, as the Juvenal and Circensian games, stage-plays, and an exhibition of gladiators. In the Juvenal, he even admitted senators and aged matrons to perform parts. In the Circensian games, he assigned the equestrian order seats apart from the rest of the people, and had races performed by chariots drawn each by four camels. In the games which he instituted for the eternal duration of the empire, and therefore ordered to be called Maximi, many of the senatorian and equestrian order, of both sexes, performed. A distinguished Roman knight descended on the stage by a rope, mounted on an elephant. A Roman play, likewise, composed by Afranius, was brought upon the stage. It was entitled, "The Fire;" and in it the performers were allowed to carry off, and to keep to themselves, the furniture of the house, which, as the plot of the play required, was burnt down in the theatre. Every day during the solemnity, many thousand articles of all descriptions were thrown amongst the people to scramble for; such as fowls of different kinds, tickets for corn, clothes, gold, silver, gems, pearls, pictures, slaves, beasts of burden, wild beasts that had been tamed; at last, ships, lots of houses, and lands, were offered as prizes in a lottery.

XII. These games he beheld from the front of the proscenium. In the show of gladiators, which he exhibited in a wooden amphitheatre, built within a year in the district of the Campus Martius, he ordered that none should be slain, not even the condemned criminals employed in the combats. He secured four hundred senators, and six hundred Roman knights, amongst whom were some of unbroken fortunes and unblemished reputation, to act as gladiators. From the same orders, he engaged persons to encounter wild beasts, and for various other services in the theatre. He presented the public with the representation of a naval fight, upon sea-water, with huge fishes swimming in it; as also with the Pyrrhic dance, performed by certain youths, to each of whom, after the performance was over, he granted the freedom of Rome. During this diversion, a bull covered Pasiphae, concealed within a wooden statue of a cow, as many of the spectators believed. Icarus, upon his first attempt to fly, fell on the stage close to the emperor's pavilion, and bespattered him with blood. For he very seldom presided in the games, but used to view them reclining on a couch, at first through some narrow apertures, but afterwards with the Podium quite open. He was the first who instituted, in imitation of the Greeks, a trial of skill in the three several exercises of music, wrestling, and horse-racing, to be performed at Rome every five years, and which he called Neronia. Upon the dedication of his bath and gymnasium, he furnished the senate and the equestrian order with oil. He appointed as judges of the trial men of consular rank, chosen by lot, who sat with the praetors. At this time he went down into the orchestra amongst the senators, and received the crown for the best performance in Latin prose and verse, for which several persons of the greatest merit contended, but they unanimously yielded to him. The crown for the best performer on the harp, being likewise awarded to him by the judges, he devoutly saluted it, and ordered it to be carried to the statue of Augustus. In the gymnastic exercises, which he presented in the Septa, while they were preparing the great sacrifice of an ox, he shaved his beard for the first time, and putting it up in a casket of gold studded with pearls of great price, consecrated it to Jupiter Capitolinus. He invited the Vestal Virgins to see the wrestlers perform, because, at Olympia, the priestesses of Ceres are allowed the privilege of witnessing that exhibition.

XIII. Amongst the spectacles presented by him, the solemn entrance of Tiridates into the city deserves to be mentioned. This personage, who was king of Armenia, he invited to Rome by very liberal promises. But being prevented by unfavourable weather from showing him to the people upon the day fixed by proclamation, he took the first opportunity which occurred; several cohorts being drawn up under arms, about the temples in the forum, while he was seated on a curule chair on the rostra, in a triumphal dress, amidst the military standards and ensigns. Upon Tiridates advancing towards him, on a stage made shelving for the purpose, he permitted him to throw himself at his feet, but quickly raised him with his right hand, and kissed him. The emperor then, at the king's request, took the turban from his head, and replaced it by a crown, whilst a person of pretorian rank proclaimed in Latin the words in which the prince addressed the emperor as a suppliant. After this ceremony, the king was conducted to the theatre, where, after renewing his obeisance, Nero seated him on his right hand. Being then greeted by universal acclamation with the title of Emperor, and sending his laurel crown to the Capitol, Nero shut the temple of the two-faced Janus, as though there now existed no war throughout the Roman empire.

XIV. He filled the consulship four times: the first for two months, the second and last for six, and the third for four; the two intermediate ones he held successively, but the others after an interval of some years between them.

XV. In the administration of justice, he scarcely ever gave his decision on the pleadings before the next day, and then in writing. His manner of hearing causes was not to allow any adjournment, but to dispatch them in order as they stood. When he withdrew to consult his assessors, he did not debate the matter openly with them; but silently and privately reading over their opinions, which they gave separately in writing, he pronounced sentence from the tribunal according to his own view of the case, as if it was the opinion of the majority. For a long time he would not admit the sons of freedmen into the senate; and those who had been admitted by former princes, he excluded from all public offices. To supernumerary candidates he gave command in the legions, to comfort them under the delay of their hopes. The consulship he commonly conferred for six months; and one of the two consuls dying a little before the first of January, he substituted no one in his place; disliking what had been formerly done for Caninius Rebilus on such an occasion, who was consul for one day only. He allowed the triumphal honours only to those who were of quaestorian rank, and to some of the equestrian order; and bestowed them without regard to military service. And instead of the quaestors, whose office it properly was, he frequently ordered that the addresses, which he sent to the senate on certain occasions, should be read by the consuls.

XVI. He devised a new style of building in the city, ordering piazzas to be erected before all houses, both in the streets and detached, to give facilities from their terraces, in case of fire, for preventing it from spreading; and these he built at his own expense. He likewise designed to extend the city walls as far as Ostia, and bring the sea from thence by a canal into the old city. Many severe regulations and new orders were made in his time. A sumptuary law was enacted. Public suppers were limited to the Sportulae; and victualling-houses restrained from selling any dressed victuals, except pulse and herbs, whereas before they sold all kinds of meat. He likewise inflicted punishments on the Christians, a sort of people who held a new and impious superstition.

He forbad the revels of the charioteers, who had long assumed a licence to stroll about, and established for themselves a kind of prescriptive right to cheat and thieve, making a jest of it. The partisans of the rival theatrical performers were banished, as well as the actors themselves.

XVII. To prevent forgery, a method was then first invented, of having writings bored, run through three times with a thread, and then sealed. It was likewise provided that in wills, the two first pages, with only the testator's name upon them, should be presented blank to those who were to sign them as witnesses; and that no one who wrote a will for another, should insert any legacy for himself. It was likewise ordained that clients should pay their advocates a certain reasonable fee, but nothing for the court, which was to be gratuitous, the charges for it being paid out of the public treasury; that causes, the cognizance of which before belonged to the judges of the exchequer, should be transferred to the forum, and the ordinary tribunals; and that all appeals from the judges should be made to the senate.

XVIII. He never entertained the least ambition or hope of augmenting and extending the frontiers of the empire. On the contrary, he had thoughts of withdrawing the troops from Britain, and was only restrained from so doing by the fear of appearing to detract from the glory of his father. All that he did was to reduce the kingdom of Pontus, which was ceded to him by Polemon, and also the Alps, upon the death of Cottius, into the form of a province.

XIX. Twice only he undertook any foreign expeditions, one to Alexandria, and the other to Achaia; but he abandoned the prosecution of the former on the very day fixed for his departure, by being deterred both by ill omens, and the hazard of the voyage. For while he was making the circuit of the temples, having seated himself in that of Vesta, when he attempted to rise, the skirt of his robe stuck fast; and he was instantly seized with such a dimness in his eyes, that he could not see a yard before him. In Achaia, he attempted to make a cut through the Isthmus; and, having made a speech encouraging his pretorians to set about the work, on a signal given by sound of trumpet, he first broke ground with a spade, and carried off a basket full of earth upon his shoulders. He made preparations for an expedition to the Pass of the Caspian mountains; forming a new legion out of his late levies in Italy, of men all six feet high, which he called the phalanx of Alexander the Great. These transactions, in part unexceptionable, and in part highly commendable, I have brought into one view, in order to separate them from the scandalous and criminal part of his conduct, of which I shall now give an account.

XX. Among the other liberal arts which he was taught in his youth, he was instructed in music; and immediately after his advancement to the empire, he sent for Terpnus, a performer upon the harp, who flourished at that time with the highest reputation. Sitting with him for several days following, as he sang and played after supper, until late at night, he began by degrees to practise upon the instrument himself. Nor did he omit any of those expedients which artists in music adopt, for the preservation and improvement of their voices. He would lie upon his back with a sheet of lead upon his breast, clear his stomach and bowels by vomits and clysters, and forbear the eating of fruits, or food prejudicial to the voice. Encouraged by his proficiency, though his voice was naturally neither loud nor clear, he was desirous of appearing upon the stage, frequently repeating amongst his friends a Greek proverb to this effect: "that no one had any regard for music which they never heard." Accordingly, he made his first public appearance at Naples; and although the theatre quivered with the sudden shock of an earthquake, he did not desist, until he had finished the piece of music he had begun. He played and sung in the same place several times, and for several days together; taking only now and then a little respite to refresh his voice. Impatient of retirement, it was his custom to go from the bath to the theatre; and after dining in the orchestra, amidst a crowded assembly of the people, he promised them in Greek, "that after he had drank a little, he would give them a tune which would make their ears tingle." Being highly pleased with the songs that were sung in his praise by some Alexandrians belonging to the fleet just arrived at Naples, he sent for more of the like singers from Alexandria. At the same time, he chose young men of the equestrian order, and above five thousand robust young fellows from the common people, on purpose to learn various kinds of applause, called bombi, imbrices, and testae, which they were to practise in his favour, whenever he performed. They were divided into several parties, and were remarkable for their fine heads of hair, and were extremely well dressed, with rings upon their left hands. The leaders of these bands had salaries of forty thousand sesterces allowed them.

XXI. At Rome also, being extremely proud of his singing, he ordered the games called Neronia to be celebrated before the time fixed for their return. All now becoming importunate to hear "his heavenly voice," he informed them, "that he would gratify those who desired it at the gardens." But the soldiers then on guard seconding the voice of the people, he promised to comply with their request immediately, and with all his heart. He instantly ordered his name to be entered upon the list of musicians who proposed to contend, and having thrown his lot into the urn among the rest, took his turn, and entered, attended by the prefects of the pretorian cohorts bearing his harp, and followed by the military tribunes, and several of his intimate friends. After he had taken his station, and made the usual prelude, he commanded Cluvius Rufus, a man of consular rank, to proclaim in the theatre, that he intended to sing the story of Niobe. This he accordingly did, and continued it until nearly ten o'clock, but deferred the disposal of the crown, and the remaining part of the solemnity, until the next year; that he might have more frequent opportunities of performing. But that being too long, he could not refrain from often appearing as a public performer during the interval. He made no scruple of exhibiting on the stage, even in the spectacles presented to the people by private persons, and was offered by one of the praetors, no less than a million of sesterces for his services. He likewise sang tragedies in a mask; the visors of the heroes and gods, as also of the heroines and goddesses, being formed into a resemblance of his own face, and that of any woman he was in love with. Amongst the rest, he sung "Canace in Labour," "Orestes the Murderer of his Mother," "Oedipus Blinded," and "Hercules Mad." In the last tragedy, it is said that a young sentinel, posted at the entrance of the stage, seeing him in a prison dress and bound with fetters, as the fable of the play required, ran to his assistance.


XXII. He had from his childhood an extravagant passion for horses; and his constant talk was of the Circensian races, notwithstanding it was prohibited him. Lamenting once, among his fellow-pupils, the case of a charioteer of the green party, who was dragged round the circus at the tail of his chariot, and being reprimanded by his tutor for it, he pretended that he was talking of Hector. In the beginning of his reign, he used to amuse himself daily with chariots drawn by four horses, made of ivory, upon a table. He attended at all the lesser exhibitions in the circus, at first privately, but at last openly; so that nobody ever doubted of his presence on any particular day. Nor did he conceal his desire to have the number of the prizes doubled; so that the races being increased accordingly, the diversion continued until a late hour; the leaders of parties refusing now to bring out their companies for any time less than the whole day. Upon this, he took a fancy for driving the chariot himself, and that even publicly. Having made his first experiment in the gardens, amidst crowds of slaves and other rabble, he at length performed in the view of all the people, in the Circus Maximus, whilst one of his freedmen dropped the napkin in the place where the magistrates used to give the signal. Not satisfied with exhibiting various specimens of his skill in those arts at Rome, he went over to Achaia, as has been already said, principally for this purpose. The several cities, in which solemn trials of musical skill used to be publicly held, had resolved to send him the crowns belonging to those who bore away the prize. These he accepted so graciously, that he not only gave the deputies who brought them an immediate audience, but even invited them to his table. Being requested by some of them to sing at supper, and prodigiously applauded, he said, "the Greeks were the only people who has an ear for music, and were the only good judges of him and his attainments." Without delay he commenced his journey, and on his arrival at Cassiope, exhibited his first musical performance before the altar of Jupiter Cassius.


XXIII. He afterwards appeared at the celebration of all public games in Greece: for such as fell in different years, he brought within the compass of one, and some he ordered to be celebrated a second time in the same year. At Olympia, likewise, contrary to custom, he appointed a public performance in music: and that he might meet with no interruption in this employment, when he was informed by his freedman Helius, that affairs at Rome required his presence, he wrote to him in these words: "Though now all your hopes and wishes are for my speedy return, yet you ought rather to advise and hope that I may come back with a character worthy of Nero." During the time of his musical performance, nobody was allowed to stir out of the theatre upon any account, however necessary; insomuch, that it is said some women with child were delivered there. Many of the spectators being quite wearied with hearing and applauding him, because the town gates were shut, slipped privately over the walls; or counterfeiting themselves dead, were carried out for their funeral. With what extreme anxiety he engaged in these contests, with what keen desire to bear away the prize, and with how much awe of the judges, is scarcely to be believed. As if his adversaries had been on a level with himself, he would watch them narrowly, defame them privately, and sometimes, upon meeting them, rail at them in very scurrilous language; or bribe them, if they were better performers than himself. He always addressed the judges with the most profound reverence before he began, telling them, "he had done all things that were necessary, by way of preparation, but that the issue of the approaching trial was in the hand of fortune; and that they, as wise and skilful men, ought to exclude from their judgment things merely accidental." Upon their encouraging him to have a good heart, he went off with more assurance, but not entirely free from anxiety; interpreting the silence and modesty of some of them into sourness and ill-nature, and saying that he was suspicious of them.


XXIV. In these contests, he adhered so strictly to the rules, that he never durst spit, nor wipe the sweat from his forehead in any other way than with his sleeve. Having, in the performance of a tragedy, dropped his sceptre, and not quickly recovering it, he was in a great fright, lest he should be set aside for the miscarriage, and could not regain his assurance, until an actor who stood by swore he was certain it had not been observed in the midst of the acclamations and exultations of the people. When the prize was adjudged to him, he always proclaimed it himself; and even entered the lists with the heralds. That no memory or the least monument might remain of any other victor in the sacred Grecian games, he ordered all their statues and pictures to be pulled down, dragged away with hooks, and thrown into the common sewers. He drove the chariot with various numbers of horses, and at the Olympic games with no fewer than ten; though, in a poem of his, he had reflected upon Mithridates for that innovation. Being thrown out of his chariot, he was again replaced, but could not retain his seat, and was obliged to give up, before he reached the goal, but was crowned notwithstanding. On his departure, he declared the whole province a free country, and conferred upon the judges in the several games the freedom of Rome, with large sums of money. All these favours he proclaimed himself with his own voice, from the middle of the Stadium, during the solemnity of the Isthmian games.


XXV. On his return from Greece, arriving at Naples, because he had commenced his career as a public performer in that city, he made his entrance in a chariot drawn by white horses through a breach in the city-wall, according to the practice of those who were victorious in the sacred Grecian games. In the same manner he entered Antium, Alba, and Rome. He made his entry into the city riding in the same chariot in which Augustus had triumphed, in a purple tunic, and a cloak embroidered with golden stars, having on his head the crown won at Olympia, and in his right hand that which was given him at the Parthian games: the rest being carried in a procession before him, with inscriptions denoting the places where they had been won, from whom, and in what plays or musical performances; whilst a train followed him with loud acclamations, crying out, that "they were the emperor's attendants, and the soldiers of his triumph." Having then caused an arch of the Circus Maximus to be taken down, he passed through the breach, as also through the Velabrum and the forum, to the Palatine hill and the temple of Apollo. Everywhere as he marched along, victims were slain, whilst the streets were strewed with saffron, and birds, chaplets, and sweetmeats scattered abroad. He suspended the sacred crowns in his chamber, about his beds, and caused statues of himself to be erected in the attire of a harper, and had his likeness stamped upon the coin in the same dress. After this period, he was so far from abating any thing of his application to music, that, for the preservation of his voice, he never addressed the soldiers but by messages, or with some person to deliver his speeches for him, when he thought fit to make his appearance amongst them. Nor did he ever do any thing either in jest or earnest, without a voice-master standing by him to caution him against overstraining his vocal organs, and to apply a handkerchief to his mouth when he did. He offered his friendship, or avowed open enmity to many, according as they were lavish or sparing in giving him their applause.

XXVI. Petulancy, lewdness, luxury, avarice, and cruelty, he practised at first with reserve and in private, as if prompted to them only by the folly of youth; but, even then, the world was of opinion that they were the faults of his nature, and not of his age. After it was dark, he used to enter the taverns disguised in a cap or a wig, and ramble about the streets in sport, which was not void of mischief. He used to beat those he met coming home from supper; and, if they made any resistance, would wound them, and throw them into the common sewer. He broke open and robbed shops; establishing an auction at home for selling his booty. In the scuffles which took place on those occasions, he often ran the hazard of losing his eyes, and even his life; being beaten almost to death by a senator, for handling his wife indecently. After this adventure, he never again ventured abroad at that time of night, without some tribunes following him at a little distance. In the day-time he would be carried to the theatre incognito in a litter, placing himself upon the upper part of the proscenium, where he not only witnessed the quarrels which arose on account of the performances, but also encouraged them. When they came to blows, and stones and pieces of broken benches began to fly about, he threw them plentifully amongst the people, and once even broke a praetor's head.

XXVII. His vices gaining strength by degrees, he laid aside his jocular amusements, and all disguise; breaking out into enormous crimes, without the least attempt to conceal them. His revels were prolonged from mid-day to midnight, while he was frequently refreshed by warm baths, and, in the summer time, by such as were cooled with snow. He often supped in public, in the Naumachia, with the sluices shut, or in the Campus Martius, or the Circus Maximus, being waited upon at table by common prostitutes of the town, and Syrian strumpets and glee-girls. As often as he went down the Tiber to Ostia, or coasted through the gulf of Baiae, booths furnished as brothels and eating-houses, were erected along the shore and river banks; before which stood matrons, who, like bawds and hostesses, allured him to land. It was also his custom to invite himself to supper with his friends; at one of which was expended no less than four millions of sesterces in chaplets, and at another something more in roses.


XXVIII. Besides the abuse of free-born lads, and the debauch of married women, he committed a rape upon Rubria, a Vestal Virgin. He was upon the point of marrying Acte, his freedwoman, having suborned some men of consular rank to swear that she was of royal descent. He gelded the boy Sporus, and endeavoured to transform him into a woman. He even went so far as to marry him, with all the usual formalities of a marriage settlement, the rose-coloured nuptial veil, and a numerous company at the wedding. When the ceremony was over, he had him conducted like a bride to his own house, and treated him as his wife. It was jocularly observed by some person, "that it would have been well for mankind, had such a wife fallen to the lot of his father Domitius." This Sporus he carried about with him in a litter round the solemn assemblies and fairs of Greece, and afterwards at Rome through the Sigillaria, dressed in the rich attire of an empress; kissing him from time to time as they rode together. That he entertained an incestuous passion for his mother, but was deterred by her enemies, for fear that this haughty and overbearing woman should, by her compliance, get him entirely into her power, and govern in every thing, was universally believed; especially after he had introduced amongst his concubines a strumpet, who was reported to have a strong resemblance to Agrippina.--------


XXIX. He prostituted his own chastity to such a degree, that after he had defiled every part of his person with some unnatural pollution, he at last invented an extraordinary kind of diversion; which was, to be let out of a den in the arena, covered with the skin of a wild beast, and then assail with violence the private parts both of men and women, while they were bound to stakes. After he had vented his furious passion upon them, he finished the play in the embraces of his freedman Doryphorus, to whom he was married in the same way that Sporus had been married to himself; imitating the cries and shrieks of young virgins, when they are ravished. I have been informed from numerous sources, that he firmly believed, no man in the world to be chaste, or any part of his person undefiled; but that most men concealed that vice, and were cunning enough to keep it secret. To those, therefore, who frankly owned their unnatural lewdness, he forgave all other crimes.

XXX. He thought there was no other use of riches and money than to squander them away profusely; regarding all those as sordid wretches who kept their expenses within due bounds; and extolling those as truly noble and generous souls, who lavished away and wasted all they possessed. He praised and admired his uncle Caius, upon no account more, than for squandering in a short time the vast treasure left him by Tiberius. Accordingly, he was himself extravagant and profuse, beyond all bounds. He spent upon Tiridates eight hundred thousand sesterces a day, a sum almost incredible; and at his departure, presented him with upwards of a million. He likewise bestowed upon Menecrates the harper, and Spicillus a gladiator, the estates and houses of men who had received the honour of a triumph. He enriched the usurer Cercopithecus Panerotes with estates both in town and country; and gave him a funeral, in pomp and magnificence little inferior to that of princes. He never wore the same garment twice. He has been known to stake four hundred thousand sesterces on a throw of the dice. It was his custom to fish with a golden net, drawn by silken cords of purple and scarlet. It is said, that he never travelled with less than a thousand baggage-carts; the mules being all shod with silver, and the drivers dressed in scarlet jackets of the finest Canusian cloth, with a numerous train of footmen, and troops of Mazacans, with bracelets on their arms, and mounted upon horses in splendid trappings.

XXXI. In nothing was he more prodigal than in his buildings. He completed his palace by continuing it from the Palatine to the Esquiline hill, calling the building at first only "The Passage," but, after it was burnt down and rebuilt, "The Golden House." Of its dimensions and furniture, it may be sufficient to say thus much: the porch was so high that there stood in it a colossal statue of himself a hundred and twenty feet in height; and the space included in it was so ample, that it had triple porticos a mile in length, and a lake like a sea, surrounded with buildings which had the appearance of a city. Within its area were corn fields, vineyards, pastures, and woods, containing a vast number of animals of various kinds, both wild and tame. In other parts it was entirely over-laid with gold, and adorned with jewels and mother of pearl. The supper rooms were vaulted, and compartments of the ceilings, inlaid with ivory, were made to revolve, and scatter flowers; while they contained pipes which shed unguents upon the guests. The chief banqueting room was circular, and revolved perpetually, night and day, in imitation of the motion of the celestial bodies. The baths were supplied with water from the sea and the Albula. Upon the dedication of this magnificent house after it was finished, all he said in approval of it was, "that he had now a dwelling fit for a man." He commenced making a pond for the reception of all the hot streams from Baiae, which he designed to have continued from Misenum to the Avernian lake, in a conduit, enclosed in galleries; and also a canal from Avernum to Ostia, that ships might pass from one to the other, without a sea voyage. The length of the proposed canal was one hundred and sixty miles; and it was intended to be of breadth sufficient to permit ships with five banks of oars to pass each other. For the execution of these designs, he ordered all prisoners, in every part of the empire, to be brought to Italy; and that even those who were convicted of the most heinous crimes, in lieu of any other sentence, should be condemned to work at them. He was encouraged to all this wild and enormous profusion, not only by the great revenue of the empire, but by the sudden hopes given him of an immense hidden treasure, which queen Dido, upon her flight from Tyre, had brought with her to Africa. This, a Roman knight pretended to assure him, upon good grounds, was still hid there in some deep caverns, and might with a little labour be recovered.

XXXII. But being disappointed in his expectations of this resource, and reduced to such difficulties, for want of money, that he was obliged to defer paying his troops, and the rewards due to the veterans; he resolved upon supplying his necessities by means of false accusations and plunder. In the first place, he ordered, that if any freedman, without sufficient reason, bore the name of the family to which he belonged; the half, instead of three fourths, of his estate should be brought into the exchequer at his decease: also that the estates of all such persons as had not in their wills been mindful of their prince, should be confiscated; and that the lawyers who had drawn or dictated such wills, should be liable to a fine. He ordained likewise, that all words and actions, upon which any informer could ground a prosecution, should be deemed treason. He demanded an equivalent for the crowns which the cities of Greece had at any time offered him in the solemn games. Having forbad any one to use the colours of amethyst and Tyrian purple, he privately sent a person to sell a few ounces of them upon the day of the Nundinae, and then shut up all the merchants' shops, on the pretext that his edict had been violated. It is said, that, as he was playing and singing in the theatre, observing a married lady dressed in the purple which he had prohibited, he pointed her out to his procurators; upon which she was immediately dragged out of her seat, and not only stripped of her clothes, but her property. He never nominated a person to any office without saying to him, "You know what I want; and let us take care that nobody has any thing he can call his own." At last he rifled many temples of the rich offerings with which they were stored, and melted down all the gold and silver statues, and amongst them those of the penates, which Galba afterwards restored.

XXXIII. He began the practice of parricide and murder with Claudius himself; for although he was not the contriver of his death, he was privy to the plot. Nor did he make any secret of it; but used afterwards to commend, in a Greek proverb, mushrooms as food fit for the gods, because Claudius had been poisoned with them. He traduced his memory both by word and deed in the grossest manner; one while charging him with folly, another while with cruelty. For he used to say by way of jest, that he had ceased morari amongst men, pronouncing the first syllable long; and treated as null many of his decrees and ordinances, as made by a doting old blockhead. He enclosed the place where his body was burnt with only a low wall of rough masonry. He attempted to poison Britannicus, as much out of envy because he had a sweeter voice, as from apprehension of what might ensue from the respect which the people entertained for his father's memory. He employed for this purpose a woman named Locusta, who had been a witness against some persons guilty of like practices. But the poison she gave him, working more slowly than he expected, and only causing a purge, he sent for the woman, and beat her with his own hand, charging her with administering an antidote instead of poison; and upon her alleging in excuse, that she had given Britannicus but a gentle mixture in order to prevent suspicion, "Think you," said he, "that I am afraid of the Julian law;" and obliged her to prepare, in his own chamber and before his eyes, as quick and strong a dose as possible. This he tried upon a kid: but the animal lingering for five hours before it expired, he ordered her to go to work again; and when she had done, he gave the poison to a pig, which dying immediately, he commanded the potion to be brought into the eating-room and given to Britannicus, while he was at supper with him. The prince had no sooner tasted it than he sunk on the floor, Nero meanwhile, pretending to the guests, that it was only a fit of the falling sickness, to which, he said, he was subject. He buried him the following day, in a mean and hurried way, during violent storms of rain. He gave Locusta a pardon, and rewarded her with a great estate in land, placing some disciples with her, to be instructed in her trade.


XXXIV. His mother being used to make strict inquiry into what he said or did, and to reprimand him with the freedom of a parent, he was so much offended, that he endeavoured to expose her to public resentment, by frequently pretending a resolution to quit the government, and retire to Rhodes. Soon afterwards, he deprived her of all honour and power, took from her the guard of Roman and German soldiers, banished her from the palace and from his society, and persecuted her in every way he could contrive; employing persons to harass her when at Rome with law-suits, and to disturb her in her retirement from town with the most scurrilous and abusive language, following her about by land and sea. But being terrified with her menaces and violent spirit, he resolved upon her destruction, and thrice attempted it by poison. Finding, however, that she had previously secured herself by antidotes, he contrived machinery, by which the floor over her bed-chamber might be made to fall upon her while she was asleep in the night. This design miscarrying likewise, through the little caution used by those who were in the secret, his next stratagem was to construct a ship which could be easily shivered, in hopes of destroying her either by drowning, or by the deck above her cabin crushing her in its fall. Accordingly, under colour of a pretended reconciliation, he wrote her an extremely affectionate letter, inviting her to Baiae, to celebrate with him the festival of Minerva. He had given private orders to the captains of the galleys which were to attend her, to shatter to pieces the ship in which she had come, by falling foul of it, but in such manner that it might appear to be done accidentally. He prolonged the entertainment, for the more convenient opportunity of executing the plot in the night; and at her return for Bauli, instead of the old ship which had conveyed her to Baiae, he offered that which he had contrived for her destruction. He attended her to the vessel in a very cheerful mood, and, at parting with her, kissed her breasts; after which he sat up very late in the night, waiting with great anxiety to learn the issue of his project. But receiving information that every thing had fallen out contrary to his wish, and that she had saved herself by swimming,--not knowing what course to take, upon her freedman, Lucius Agerinus bringing word, with great joy, that she was safe and well, he privately dropped a poniard by him. He then commanded the freedman to be seized and put in chains, under pretence of his having been employed by his mother to assassinate him; at the same time ordering her to be put to death, and giving out, that, to avoid punishment for her intended crime, she had laid violent hands upon herself. Other circumstances, still more horrible, are related on good authority; as that he went to view her corpse, and handling her limbs, pointed out some blemishes, and commended other points; and that, growing thirsty during the survey, he called for drink. Yet he was never afterwards able to bear the stings of his own conscience for this atrocious act, although encouraged by the congratulatory addresses of the army, the senate, and people. He frequently affirmed that he was haunted by his mother's ghost, and persecuted with the whips and burning torches of the Furies. Nay, he attempted by magical rites to bring up her ghost from below, and soften her rage against him. When he was in Greece, he durst not attend the celebration of the Eleusinian mysteries, at the initiation of which, impious and wicked persons are warned by the voice of the herald from approaching the rites. Besides the murder of his mother, he had been guilty of that of his aunt; for, being obliged to keep her bed in consequence of a complaint in her bowels, he paid her a visit, and she, being then advanced in years, stroking his downy chin, in the tenderness of affection, said to him: "May I but live to see the day when this is shaved for the first time, and I shall then die contented." He turned, however, to those about him, made a jest of it, saying, that he would have his beard immediately taken off, and ordered the physicians to give her more violent purgatives. He seized upon her estate before she had expired; suppressing her will, that he might enjoy the whole himself.


XXXV. He had, besides Octavia, two other wives: Poppaea Sabina, whose father had borne the office of quaestor, and who had been married before to a Roman knight: and, after her, Statilia Messalina, great-grand-daughter of Taurus who was twice consul, and received the honour of a triumph. To obtain possession of her, he put to death her husband, Atticus Vestinus, who was then consul. He soon became disgusted with Octavia, and ceased from having any intercourse with her; and being censured by his friends for it, he replied, "She ought to be satisfied with having the rank and appendages of his wife." Soon afterwards, he made several attempts, but in vain, to strangle her, and then divorced her for barrenness. But the people, disapproving of the divorce, and making severe comments upon it, he also banished her. At last he put her to death, upon a charge of adultery, so impudent and false, that, when all those who were put to the torture positively denied their knowledge of it, he suborned his pedagogue, Anicetus, to affirm, that he had secretly intrigued with and debauched her. He married Poppaea twelve days after the divorce of Octavia, and entertained a great affection for her; but, nevertheless, killed her with a kick which he gave her when she was big with child, and in bad health, only because she found fault with him for returning late from driving his chariot. He had by her a daughter, Claudia Augusta, who died an infant. There was no person at all connected with him who escaped his deadly and unjust cruelty. Under pretence of her being engaged in a plot against him, he put to death Antonia, Claudius's daughter, who refused to marry him after the death of Poppaea. In the same way, he destroyed all who were allied to him either by blood or marriage; amongst whom was young Aulus Plautinus. He first compelled him to submit to his unnatural lust, and then ordered him to be executed, crying out, "Let my mother bestow her kisses on my successor thus defiled;" pretending that he had been his mothers paramour, and by her encouraged to aspire to the empire. His step-son, Rufinus Crispinus, Poppaea's son, though a minor, he ordered to be drowned in the sea, while he was fishing, by his own slaves, because he was reported to act frequently amongst his play-fellows the part of a general or an emperor. He banished Tuscus, his nurse's son, for presuming, when he was procurator of Egypt, to wash in the baths which had been constructed in expectation of his own coming. Seneca, his preceptor, he forced to kill himself, though, upon his desiring leave to retire, and offering to surrender his estate, he solemnly swore, "that there was no foundation for his suspicions, and that he would perish himself sooner than hurt him." Having promised Burrhus, the pretorian prefect, a remedy for a swelling in his throat, he sent him poison. Some old rich freedmen of Claudius, who had formerly not only promoted his adoption, but were also instrumental to his advancement to the empire, and had been his governors, he took off by poison given them in their meat or drink.


XXXVI. Nor did he proceed with less cruelty against those who were not of his family. A blazing star, which is vulgarly supposed to portend destruction to kings and princes, appeared above the horizon several nights successively. He felt great anxiety on account of this phenomenon, and being informed by one Babilus, an astrologer, that princes were used to expiate such omens by the sacrifice of illustrious persons, and so avert the danger foreboded to their own persons, by bringing it on the heads of their chief men, he resolved on the destruction of the principal nobility in Rome. He was the more encouraged to this, because he had some plausible pretence for carrying it into execution, from the discovery of two conspiracies against him; the former and more dangerous of which was that formed by Piso, and discovered at Rome; the other was that of Vinicius, at Beneventum. The conspirators were brought to their trials loaded with triple fetters. Some ingenuously confessed the charge; others avowed that they thought the design against his life an act of favour for which he was obliged to them, as it was impossible in any other way than by death to relieve a person rendered infamous by crimes of the greatest enormity. The children of those who had been condemned, were banished the city, and afterwards either poisoned or starved to death. It is asserted that some of them, with their tutors, and the slaves who carried their satchels, were all poisoned together at one dinner; and others not suffered to seek their daily bread.

XXXVII. From this period he butchered, without distinction or quarter, all whom his caprice suggested as objects for his cruelty; and upon the most frivolous pretences. To mention only a few: Salvidienus Orfitus was accused of letting out three taverns attached to his house in the Forum to some cities for the use of their deputies at Rome. The charge against Cassius Longinus, a lawyer who had lost his sight, was, that he kept amongst the busts of his ancestors that of Caius Cassius, who was concerned in the death of Julius Caesar. The only charge objected against Paetus Thrasea was, that he had a melancholy cast of features, and looked like a schoolmaster. He allowed but one hour to those whom he obliged to kill themselves; and, to prevent delay, he sent them physicians "to cure them immediately, if they lingered beyond that time;" for so he called bleeding them to death. There was at that time an Egyptian of a most voracious appetite, who would digest raw flesh, or any thing else that was given him. It was credibly reported, that the emperor was extremely desirous of furnishing him with living men to tear and devour. Being elated with his great success in the perpetration of crimes, he declared, "that no prince before himself ever knew the extent of his power." He threw out strong intimations that he would not even spare the senators who survived, but would entirely extirpate that order, and put the provinces and armies into the hands of the Roman knights and his own freedmen. It is certain that he never gave or vouchsafed to allow any one the customary kiss, either on entering or departing, or even returned a salute. And at the inauguration of a work, the cut through the Isthmus, he, with a loud voice, amidst the assembled multitude, uttered a prayer, that "the undertaking might prove fortunate for himself and the Roman people," without taking the smallest notice of the senate.

XXXVIII. He spared, moreover, neither the people of Rome, nor the capital of his country. Somebody in conversation saying--

Emou thanontos gaia michthaeto pyri When I am dead let fire devour the world--

"Nay," said he, "let it be while I am living" [emou xontos]. And he acted accordingly: for, pretending to be disgusted with the old buildings, and the narrow and winding streets, he set the city on fire so openly, that many of consular rank caught his own household servants on their property with tow, and torches in their hands, but durst not meddle with them. There being near his Golden House some granaries, the site of which he exceedingly coveted, they were battered as if with machines of war, and set on fire, the walls being built of stone. During six days and seven nights this terrible devastation continued, the people being obliged to fly to the tombs and monuments for lodging and shelter. Meanwhile, a vast number of stately buildings, the houses of generals celebrated in former times, and even then still decorated with the spoils of war, were laid in ashes; as well as the temples of the gods, which had been vowed and dedicated by the kings of Rome, and afterwards in the Punic and Gallic wars: in short, everything that was remarkable and worthy to be seen which time had spared. This fire he beheld from a tower in the house of Mecaenas, and "being greatly delighted," as he said, "with the beautiful effects of the conflagration," he sung a poem on the ruin of Troy, in the tragic dress he used on the stage. To turn this calamity to his own advantage by plunder and rapine, he promised to remove the bodies of those who had perished in the fire, and clear the rubbish at his own expense; suffering no one to meddle with the remains of their property. But he not only received, but exacted contributions on account of the loss, until he had exhausted the means both of the provinces and private persons.

XXXIX. To these terrible and shameful calamities brought upon the people by their prince, were added some proceeding from misfortune. Such were a pestilence, by which, within the space of one autumn, there died no less than thirty thousand persons, as appeared from the registers in the temple of Libitina; a great disaster in Britain, where two of the principal towns belonging to the Romans were plundered; and a dreadful havoc made both amongst our troops and allies; a shameful discomfiture of the army of the East; where, in Armenia, the legions were obliged to pass under the yoke, and it was with great difficulty that Syria was retained. Amidst all these disasters, it was strange, and, indeed, particularly remarkable, that he bore nothing more patiently than the scurrilous language and railing abuse which was in every one's mouth; treating no class of persons with more gentleness, than those who assailed him with invective and lampoons. Many things of that kind were posted up about the city, or otherwise published, both in Greek and Latin: such as these,

Neron, Orestaes, Alkmaion, maetroktonai. Neonymphon Neron, idian maeter apekteinen.

Orestes and Alcaeon--Nero too, The lustful Nero, worst of all the crew, Fresh from his bridal-- their own mothers slew.

Quis neget Aeneae magna de stirpe Neronem? Sustulit hic matrem: sustulit ille patrem.

Sprung from Aeneas, pious, wise and great, Who says that Nero is degenerate? Safe through the flames, one bore his sire; the other, To save himself, took off his loving mother.

Dum tendit citharam noster, dum cornua Parthus, Noster erit Paean, ille Ekataebeletaes.

His lyre to harmony our Nero strings; His arrows o'er the plain the Parthian wings: Ours call the tuneful Paean,--famed in war, The other Phoebus name, the god who shoots afar.

Roma domus fiet: Vejos migrate, Quirites, Si non et Vejos occupat ista domus.

All Rome will be one house: to Veii fly, Should it not stretch to Veii, by and by.

But he neither made any inquiry after the authors, nor when information was laid before the senate against some of them, would he allow a severe sentence to be passed. Isidorus, the Cynic philosopher, said to him aloud, as he was passing along the streets, "You sing the misfortunes of Nauplius well, but behave badly yourself." And Datus, a comic actor, when repeating these words in the piece, "Farewell, father! Farewell mother!" mimicked the gestures of persons drinking and swimming, significantly alluding to the deaths of Claudius and Agrippina: and on uttering the last clause,

Orcus vobis ducit pedes; You stand this moment on the brink of Orcus;

he plainly intimated his application of it to the precarious position of the senate. Yet Nero only banished the player and philosopher from the city and Italy; either because he was insensible to shame, or from apprehension that if he discovered his vexation, still keener things might be said of him.

XL. The world, after tolerating such an emperor for little less than fourteen years, at length forsook him; the Gauls, headed by Julius Vindex, who at that time governed the province as pro-praetor, being the first to revolt. Nero had been formerly told by astrologers, that it would be his fortune to be at last deserted by all the world; and this occasioned that celebrated saying of his, "An artist can live in any country;" by which he meant to offer as an excuse for his practice of music, that it was not only his amusement as a prince, but might be his support when reduced to a private station. Yet some of the astrologers promised him, in his forlorn state, the rule of the East, and some in express words the kingdom of Jerusalem. But the greater part of them flattered him with assurances of his being restored to his former fortune. And being most inclined to believe the latter prediction, upon losing Britain and Armenia, he imagined he had run through all the misfortunes which the fates had decreed him. But when, upon consulting the oracle of Apollo at Delphi, he was advised to beware of the seventy-third year, as if he were not to die till then, never thinking of Galba's age, he conceived such hopes, not only of living to advanced years, but of constant and singular good fortune, that having lost some things of great value by shipwreck, he scrupled not to say amongst his friends, that "the fishes would bring them back to him." At Naples he heard of the insurrection in Gaul, on the anniversary of the day on which he killed his mother, and bore it with so much unconcern, as to excite a suspicion that he was really glad of it, since he had now a fair opportunity of plundering those wealthy provinces by the right of war. Immediately going to the gymnasium, he witnessed the exercise of the wrestlers with the greatest delight. Being interrupted at supper with letters which brought yet worse news, he expressed no greater resentment, than only to threaten the rebels. For eight days together, he never attempted to answer any letters, nor give any orders, but buried the whole affair in profound silence.

XLI. Being roused at last by numerous proclamations of Vindex, treating him with reproaches and contempt, he in a letter to the senate exhorted them to avenge his wrongs and those of the republic; desiring them to excuse his not appearing in the senate-house, because he had got cold. But nothing so much galled him, as to find himself railed at as a pitiful harper, and, instead of Nero, styled Aenobarbus: which being his family name, since he was upbraided with it, he declared that he would resume it, and lay aside the name he had taken by adoption. Passing by the other accusations as wholly groundless, he earnestly refuted that of his want of skill in an art upon which he had bestowed so much pains, and in which he had arrived at such perfection; asking frequently those about him, "if they knew any one who was a more accomplished musician?" But being alarmed by messengers after messengers of ill news from Gaul, he returned in great consternation to Rome. On the road, his mind was somewhat relieved, by observing the frivolous omen of a Gaulish soldier defeated and dragged by the hair by a Roman knight, which was sculptured on a monument; so that he leaped for joy, and adored the heavens. Even then he made no appeal either to the senate or people, but calling together some of the leading men at his own house, he held a hasty consultation upon the present state of affairs, and then, during the remainder of the day, carried them about with him to view some musical instruments, of a new invention, which were played by water exhibiting all the parts, and discoursing upon the principles and difficulties of the contrivance; which, he told them, he intended to produce in the theatre, if Vindex would give him leave.

XLII. Soon afterwards, he received intelligence that Galba and the Spaniards had declared against him; upon which, he fainted, and losing his reason, lay a long time speechless, apparently dead. As soon as recovered from this state stupefaction he tore his clothes, and beat his head, crying out, "It is all over with me!" His nurse endeavouring to comfort him, and telling him that the like things had happened to other princes before him, he replied, "I am beyond all example wretched, for I have lost an empire whilst I am still living." He, nevertheless, abated nothing of his luxury and inattention to business. Nay, on the arrival of good news from the provinces, he, at a sumptuous entertainment, sung with an air of merriment, some jovial verses upon the leaders of the revolt, which were made public; and accompanied them with suitable gestures. Being carried privately to the theatre, he sent word to an actor who was applauded by the spectators, "that he had it all his own way, now that he himself did not appear on the stage."

XLIII. At the first breaking out of these troubles, it is believed that he had formed many designs of a monstrous nature, although conformable enough to his natural disposition. These were to send new governors and commanders to the provinces and the armies, and employ assassins to butcher all the former governors and commanders, as men unanimously engaged in a conspiracy against him; to massacre the exiles in every quarter, and all the Gaulish population in Rome; the former lest they should join the insurrection; the latter as privy to the designs of their countrymen, and ready to support them; to abandon Gaul itself, to be wasted and plundered by his armies; to poison the whole senate at a feast; to fire the city, and then let loose the wild beasts upon the people, in order to impede their stopping the progress of the flames. But being deterred from the execution of these designs not so much by remorse of conscience, as by despair of being able to effect them, and judging an expedition into Gaul necessary, he removed the consuls from their office, before the time of its expiration was arrived; and in their room assumed the consulship himself without a colleague, as if the fates had decreed that Gaul should not be conquered, but by a consul. Upon assuming the fasces, after an entertainment at the palace, as he walked out of the room leaning on the arms of some of his friends, he declared, that as soon as he arrived in the province, he would make his appearance amongst the troops, unarmed, and do nothing but weep: and that, after he had brought the mutineers to repentance, he would, the next day, in the public rejoicings, sing songs of triumph, which he must now, without loss of time, apply himself to compose.

XLIV. In preparing for this expedition, his first care was to provide carriages for his musical instruments and machinery to be used upon the stage; to have the hair of the concubines he carried with him dressed in the fashion of men; and to supply them with battle-axes, and Amazonian bucklers. He summoned the city-tribes to enlist; but no qualified persons appearing, he ordered all masters to send a certain number of slaves, the best they had, not excepting their stewards and secretaries. He commanded the several orders of the people to bring in a fixed proportion of their estates, as they stood in the censor's books; all tenants of houses and mansions to pay one year's rent forthwith into the exchequer; and, with unheard-of strictness, would receive only new coin of the purest silver and the finest gold; insomuch that most people refused to pay, crying out unanimously that he ought to squeeze the informers, and oblige them to surrender their gains.

XLV. The general odium in which he was held received an increase by the great scarcity of corn, and an occurrence connected with it. For, as it happened just at that time, there arrived from Alexandria a ship, which was said to be freighted with dust for the wrestlers belonging to the emperor. This so much inflamed the public rage, that he was treated with the utmost abuse and scurrility. Upon the top of one of his statues was placed the figure of a chariot with a Greek inscription, that "Now indeed he had a race to run; let him be gone." A little bag was tied about another, with a ticket containing these words; "What could I do?"--"Truly thou hast merited the sack." Some person likewise wrote on the pillars in the forum, "that he had even woke the cocks with his singing." And many, in the night-time, pretending to find fault with their servants, frequently called for a Vindex.

XLVI. He was also terrified with manifest warnings, both old and new, arising from dreams, auspices, and omens. He had never been used to dream before the murder of his mother. After that event, he fancied in his sleep that he was steering a ship, and that the rudder was forced from him: that he was dragged by his wife Octavia into a prodigiously dark place; and was at one time covered over with a vast swarm of winged ants, and at another, surrounded by the national images which were set up near Pompey's theatre, and hindered from advancing farther; that a Spanish jennet he was fond of, had his hinder parts so changed, as to resemble those of an ape; and having his head only left unaltered, neighed very harmoniously. The doors of the mausoleum of Augustus flying open of themselves, there issued from it a voice, calling on him by name. The Lares being adorned with fresh garlands on the calends (the first) of January, fell down during the preparations for sacrificing to them. While he was taking the omens, Sporus presented him with a ring, the stone of which had carved upon it the Rape of Proserpine. When a great multitude of the several orders was assembled, to attend at the solemnity of making vows to the gods, it was a long time before the keys of the Capitol could be found. And when, in a speech of his to the senate against Vindex, these words were read, "that the miscreants should be punished and soon make the end they merited," they all cried out, "You will do it, Augustus." It was likewise remarked, that the last tragic piece which he sung, was Oedipus in Exile, and that he fell as he was repeating this verse:

Thanein m' anoge syngamos, maetaer, pataer. Wife, mother, father, force me to my end.

XLVII. Meanwhile, on the arrival of the news, that the rest of the armies had declared against him, he tore to pieces the letters which were delivered to him at dinner, overthrew the table, and dashed with violence against the ground two favourite cups, which he called Homer's, because some of that poet's verses were cut upon them. Then taking from Locusta a dose of poison, which he put up in a golden box, he went into the Servilian gardens, and thence dispatching a trusty freedman to Ostia, with orders to make ready a fleet, he endeavoured to prevail with some tribunes and centurions of the pretorian guards to attend him in his flight; but part of them showing no great inclination to comply, others absolutely refusing, and one of them crying out aloud,

Usque adeone mori miserum est? Say, is it then so sad a thing to die?

he was in great perplexity whether he should submit himself to Galba, or apply to the Parthians for protection, or else appear before the people dressed in mourning, and, upon the rostra, in the most piteous manner, beg pardon for his past misdemeanors, and, if he could not prevail, request of them to grant him at least the government of Egypt. A speech to this purpose was afterwards found in his writing-case. But it is conjectured that he durst not venture upon this project, for fear of being torn to pieces, before he could get to the Forum. Deferring, therefore, his resolution until the next day, he awoke about midnight, and finding the guards withdrawn, he leaped out of bed, and sent round for his friends. But none of them vouchsafing any message in reply, he went with a few attendants to their houses. The doors being every where shut, and no one giving him any answer, he returned to his bed-chamber; whence those who had the charge of it had all now eloped; some having gone one way, and some another, carrying off with them his bedding and box of poison. He then endeavoured to find Spicillus, the gladiator, or some one to kill him; but not being able to procure any one, "What!" said he, "have I then neither friend nor foe?" and immediately ran out, as if he would throw himself into the Tiber.

XLVIII. But this furious impulse subsiding, he wished for some place of privacy, where he might collect his thoughts; and his freedman Phaon offering him his country-house, between the Salarian and Nomentan roads, about four miles from the city, he mounted a horse, barefoot as he was, and in his tunic, only slipping over it an old soiled cloak; with his head muffled up, and an handkerchief before his face, and four persons only to attend him, of whom Sporus was one. He was suddenly struck with horror by an earthquake, and by a flash of lightning which darted full in his face, and heard from the neighbouring camp the shouts of the soldiers, wishing his destruction, and prosperity to Galba. He also heard a traveller they met on the road, say, "They are in pursuit of Nero:" and another ask, "Is there any news in the city about Nero?" Uncovering his face when his horse was started by the scent of a carcase which lay in the road, he was recognized and saluted by an old soldier who had been discharged from the guards. When they came to the lane which turned up to the house, they quitted their horses, and with much difficulty he wound among bushes, and briars, and along a track through a bed of rushes, over which they spread their cloaks for him to walk on. Having reached a wall at the back of the villa, Phaon advised him to hide himself awhile in a sand-pit; when he replied, "I will not go under-ground alive." Staying there some little time, while preparations were made for bringing him privately into the villa, he took up some water out of a neighbouring tank in his hand, to drink, saying, "This is Nero's distilled water." Then his cloak having been torn by the brambles, he pulled out the thorns which stuck in it. At last, being admitted, creeping upon his hands and knees, through a hole made for him in the wall, he lay down in the first closet he came to, upon a miserable pallet, with an old coverlet thrown over it; and being both hungry and thirsty, though he refused some coarse bread that was brought him, he drank a little warm water.

XLIX. All who surrounded him now pressing him to save himself from the indignities which were ready to befall him, he ordered a pit to be sunk before his eyes, of the size of his body, and the bottom to be covered with pieces of marble put together, if any could be found about the house; and water and wood, to be got ready for immediate use about his corpse; weeping at every thing that was done, and frequently saying, "What an artist is now about to perish!" Meanwhile, letters being brought in by a servant belonging to Phaon, he snatched them out of his hand, and there read, "That he had been declared an enemy by the senate, and that search was making for him, that he might be punished according to the ancient custom of the Romans." He then inquired what kind of punishment that was; and being told, that the practice was to strip the criminal naked, and scourge him to death, while his neck was fastened within a forked stake, he was so terrified that he took up two daggers which he had brought with him, and after feeling the points of both, put them up again, saying, "The fatal hour is not yet come." One while, he begged of Sporus to begin to wail and lament; another while, he entreated that one of them would set him an example by killing himself; and then again, he condemned his own want of resolution in these words: "I yet live to my shame and disgrace: this is not becoming for Nero: it is not becoming. Thou oughtest in such circumstances to have a good heart: Come, then: courage, man!" The horsemen who had received orders to bring him away alive, were now approaching the house. As soon as he heard them coming, he uttered with a trembling voice the following verse,

Hippon m' okupodon amphi ktupos ouata ballei; The noise of swift-heel'd steeds assails my ears;

he drove a dagger into his throat, being assisted in the act by Epaphroditus, his secretary. A centurion bursting in just as he was half-dead, and applying his cloak to the wound, pretending that he was come to his assistance, he made no other reply but this, "'Tis too late;" and "Is this your loyalty?" Immediately after pronouncing these words, he expired, with his eyes fixed and starting out of his head, to the terror of all who beheld him. He had requested of his attendants, as the most essential favour, that they would let no one have his head, but that by all means his body might be burnt entire. And this, Icelus, Galba's freedman, granted. He had but a little before been discharged from the prison into which he had been thrown, when the disturbances first broke out.

L. The expenses of his funeral amounted to two hundred thousand sesterces; the bed upon which his body was carried to the pile and burnt, being covered with the white robes, interwoven with gold, which he had worn upon the calends of January preceding. His nurses, Ecloge and Alexandra, with his concubine Acte, deposited his remains in the tomb belonging to the family of the Domitii, which stands upon the top of the Hill of the Gardens, and is to be seen from the Campus Martius. In that monument, a coffin of porphyry, with an altar of marble of Luna over it, is enclosed by a wall built of stone brought from Thasos.

LI. In stature he was a little below the common height; his skin was foul and spotted; his hair inclined to yellow; his features were agreeable, rather than handsome; his eyes grey and dull, his neck was thick, his belly prominent, his legs very slender, his constitution sound. For, though excessively luxurious in his mode of living, he had, in the course of fourteen years, only three fits of sickness; which were so slight, that he neither forbore the use of wine, nor made any alteration in his usual diet. In his dress, and the care of his person, he was so careless, that he had his hair cut in rings, one above another; and when in Achaia, he let it grow long behind; and he generally appeared in public in the loose dress which he used at table, with a handkerchief about his neck, and without either a girdle or shoes.

LII. He was instructed, when a boy, in the rudiments of almost all the liberal sciences; but his mother diverted him from the study of philosophy, as unsuited to one destined to be an emperor; and his preceptor, Seneca, discouraged him from reading the ancient orators, that he might longer secure his devotion to himself. Therefore, having a turn for poetry, he composed verses both with pleasure and ease; nor did he, as some think, publish those of other writers as his own. Several little pocket-books and loose sheets have cone into my possession, which contain some well-known verses in his own hand, and written in such a manner, that it was very evident, from the blotting and interlining, that they had not been transcribed from a copy, nor dictated by another, but were written by the composer of them.

LIII. He had likewise great taste for drawing and painting, as well as for moulding statues in plaster. But, above all things, he most eagerly coveted popularity, being the rival of every man who obtained the applause of the people for any thing he did. It was the general belief, that, after the crowns he won by his performances on the stage, he would the next lustrum have taken his place among the wrestlers at the Olympic games. For he was continually practising that art; nor did he witness the gymnastic games in any part of Greece otherwise than sitting upon the ground in the stadium, as the umpires do. And if a pair of wrestlers happened to break the bounds, he would with his own hands drag them back into the centre of the circle. Because he was thought to equal Apollo in music, and the sun in chariot-driving, he resolved also to imitate the achievements of Hercules. And they say that a lion was got ready for him to kill, either with a club, or with a close hug, in view of the people in the amphitheatre; which he was to perform naked.

LIV. Towards the end of his life, he publicly vowed, that if his power in the state was securely re-established, he would, in the spectacles which he intended to exhibit in honour of his success, include a performance upon organs, as well as upon flutes and bagpipes, and, on the last day of the games, would act in the play, and take the part of Turnus, as we find it in Virgil. And there are some who say, that he put to death the player Paris as a dangerous rival.

LV. He had an insatiable desire to immortalize his name, and acquire a reputation which should last through all succeeding ages; but it was capriciously directed. He therefore took from several things and places their former appellations, and gave them new names derived from his own. He called the month of April, Neroneus, and designed changing the name of Rome into that of Neropolis.

LVI. He held all religious rites in contempt, except those of the Syrian Goddess; but at last he paid her so little reverence, that he made water upon her; being now engaged in another superstition, in which only he obstinately persisted. For having received from some obscure plebeian a little image of a girl, as a preservative against plots, and discovering a conspiracy immediately after, he constantly worshipped his imaginary protectress as the greatest amongst the gods, offering to her three sacrifices daily. He was also desirous to have it supposed that he had, by revelations from this deity, a knowledge of future events. A few months before he died, he attended a sacrifice, according to the Etruscan rites, but the omens were not favourable.

LVII. He died in the thirty-second year of his age, upon the same day on which he had formerly put Octavia to death; and the public joy was so great upon the occasion, that the common people ran about the city with caps upon their heads. Some, however, were not wanting, who for a long time decked his tomb with spring and summer flowers. Sometimes they placed his image upon the rostra, dressed in robes of state; at another, they published proclamations in his name, as if he were still alive, and would shortly return to Rome, and take vengeance on all his enemies. Vologesus, king of the Parthians, when he sent ambassadors to the senate to renew his alliance with the Roman people, earnestly requested that due honour should be paid to the memory of Nero; and, to conclude, when, twenty years afterwards, at which time I was a young man, some person of obscure birth gave himself out for Nero, that name secured him so favourable a reception from the Parthians, that he was very zealously supported, and it was with much difficulty that they were prevailed upon to give him up.

\* \* \* \* \* \*

Though no law had ever passed for regulating the transmission of the imperial power, yet the design of conveying it by lineal descent was implied in the practice of adoption. By the rule of hereditary succession, Britannicus, the son of Claudius, was the natural heir to the throne; but he was supplanted by the artifices of his stepmother, who had the address to procure it for her own son, Nero. From the time of Augustus it had been the custom of each of the new sovereigns to commence his reign in such a manner as tended to acquire popularity, however much they all afterwards degenerated from those specious beginnings. Whether this proceeded entirely from policy, or that nature was not yet vitiated by the intoxication of uncontrolled power, is uncertain; but such were the excesses into which they afterwards plunged, that we can scarcely exempt any of them, except, perhaps, Claudius, from the imputation of great original depravity. The vicious temper of Tiberius was known to his own mother, Livia; that of Caligula had been obvious to those about him from his infancy; Claudius seems to have had naturally a stronger tendency to weakness than to vice; but the inherent wickedness of Nero was discovered at an early period by his preceptor, Seneca. Yet even this emperor commenced his reign in a manner which procured him approbation. Of all the Roman emperors who had hitherto reigned, he seems to have been most corrupted by profligate favourites, who flattered his follies and vices, to promote their own aggrandisement. In the number of these was Tigellinus, who met at last with the fate which he had so amply merited.

The several reigns from the death of Augustus present us with uncommon scenes of cruelty and horror; but it was reserved for that of Nero to exhibit to the world the atrocious act of an emperor deliberately procuring the death of his mother.

Julia Agrippina was the daughter of Germanicus, and married Domitius Aenobarbus, by whom she had Nero. At the death of Messalina she was a widow; and Claudius, her uncle, entertaining a design of entering again into the married state, she aspired to an incestuous alliance with him, in competition with Lollia Paulina, a woman of beauty and intrigue, who had been married to C. Caesar. The two rivals were strongly supported by their respective parties; but Agrippina, by her superior interest with the emperor's favourites, and the familiarity to which her near relation gave her a claim, obtained the preference; and the portentous nuptials of the emperor and his niece were publicly solemnized in the palace. Whether she was prompted to this flagrant indecency by personal ambition alone, or by the desire of procuring the succession to the empire for her son, is uncertain; but there remains no doubt of her having removed Claudius by poison, with a view to the object now mentioned. Besides Claudius, she projected the death of L. Silanus, and she accomplished that of his brother, Junius Silanus, by means likewise of poison. She appears to have been richly endowed with the gifts of nature, but in her disposition intriguing, violent, imperious, and ready to sacrifice every principle of virtue, in the pursuit of supreme power or sensual gratification. As she resembled Livia in the ambition of a mother, and the means by which she indulged it, so she more than equalled her in the ingratitude of an unnatural son and a parricide. She is said to have left behind her some memoirs, of which Tacitus availed himself in the composition of his Annals.

In this reign, the conquest of the Britons still continued to be the principal object of military enterprise, and Suetonius Paulinus was invested with the command of the Roman army employed in the reduction of that people. The island of Mona, now Anglesey, being the chief seat of the Druids, he resolved to commence his operations with attacking a place which was the centre of superstition, and to which the vanquished Britons retreated as the last asylum of liberty. The inhabitants endeavoured, both by force of arms and the terrors of religion, to obstruct his landing on this sacred island. The women and Druids assembled promiscuously with the soldiers upon the shore, where running about in wild disorder, with flaming torches in their hands, and pouring forth the most hideous exclamations, they struck the Romans with consternation. But Suetonius animating his troops, they boldly attacked the inhabitants, routed them in the field, and burned the Druids in the same fires which had been prepared by those priests for the catastrophe of the invaders, destroying at the same time all the consecrated groves and altars in the island. Suetonius having thus triumphed over the religion of the Britons, flattered himself with the hopes of soon effecting the reduction of the people. But they, encouraged by his absence, had taken arms, and under the conduct of Boadicea, queen of the Iceni, who had been treated in the most ignominious manner by the Roman tribunes, had already driven the hateful invaders from their several settlements. Suetonius hastened to the protection of London, which was by this time a flourishing Roman colony; but he found upon his arrival, that any attempt to preserve it would be attended with the utmost danger to the army. London therefore was reduced to ashes; and the Romans, and all strangers, to the number of seventy thousand, were put to the sword without distinction, the Britons seeming determined to convince the enemy that they would acquiesce in no other terms than a total evacuation of the island. This massacre, however, was revenged by Suetonius in a decisive engagement, where eighty thousand of the Britons are said to have been killed; after which, Boadicea, to avoid falling into the hands of the insolent conquerors, put a period to her own life by means of poison. It being judged unadvisable that Suetonius should any longer conduct the war against a people whom he had exasperated by his severity, he was recalled, and Petronius Turpilianus appointed in his room. The command was afterwards given successively to Trebellius Maximus and Vettius Bolanus; but the plan pursued by these generals was only to retain, by a conciliatory administration, the parts of the island which had already submitted to the Roman arms.

During these transactions in Britain, Nero himself was exhibiting, in Rome or some of the provinces, such scenes of extravagance as almost exceed credibility. In one place, entering the lists amongst the competitors in a chariot race; in another, contending for victory with the common musicians on the stage; revelling in open day in the company of the most abandoned prostitutes and the vilest of men; in the night, committing depredations on the peaceful inhabitants of the capital; polluting with detestable lust, or drenching with human blood, the streets, the palace, and the habitations of private families; and, to crown his enormities, setting fire to Rome, while he sung with delight in beholding the dreadful conflagration. In vain would history be ransacked for a parallel to this emperor, who united the most shameful vices to the most extravagant vanity, the most abject meanness to the strongest but most preposterous ambition; and the whole of whose life was one continued scene of lewdness, sensuality, rapine, cruelty, and folly. It is emphatically observed by Tacitus, "that Nero, after the murder of many illustrious personages, manifested a desire of extirpating virtue itself."

Among the excesses of Nero's reign, are to be mentioned the horrible cruelties exercised against the Christians in various parts of the empire, in which inhuman transactions the natural barbarity of the emperor was inflamed by the prejudices and interested policy of the pagan priesthood.

The tyrant scrupled not to charge them with the act of burning Rome; and he satiated his fury against them by such outrages as are unexampled in history. They were covered with the skins of wild beasts, and torn by dogs; were crucified, and set on fire, that they might serve for lights in the night-time. Nero offered his gardens for this spectacle, and exhibited the games of the Circus by this dreadful illumination. Sometimes they were covered with wax and other combustible materials, after which a sharp stake was put under their chin, to make them stand upright, and they were burnt alive, to give light to the spectators.

In the person of Nero, it is observed by Suetonius, the race of the Caesars became extinct; a race rendered illustrious by the first and second emperors, but which their successors no less disgraced. The despotism of Julius Caesar, though haughty and imperious, was liberal and humane: that of Augustus, if we exclude a few instances of vindictive severity towards individuals, was mild and conciliating; but the reigns of Tiberius, Caligula, and Nero (for we except Claudius from part of the censure), while discriminated from each other by some peculiar circumstances, exhibited the most flagrant acts of licentiousness and perverted authority. The most abominable lust, the most extravagant luxury, the most shameful rapaciousness, and the most inhuman cruelty, constitute the general characteristics of those capricious and detestable tyrants. Repeated experience now clearly refuted the opinion of Augustus, that he had introduced amongst the Romans the best form of government: but while we make this observation, it is proper to remark, that, had he even restored the republic, there is reason to believe that the nation would again have been soon distracted with internal divisions, and a perpetual succession of civil wars. The manners of the people were become too dissolute to be restrained by the authority of elective and temporary magistrates; and the Romans were hastening to that fatal period when general and great corruption, with its attendant debility, would render them an easy prey to any foreign invaders.

But the odious government of the emperors was not the only grievance under which the people laboured in those disastrous times: patrician avarice concurred with imperial rapacity to increase the sufferings of the nation. The senators, even during the commonwealth, had become openly corrupt in the dispensation of public justice; and under the government of the emperors pernicious abuse was practised to a yet greater extent. That class being now, equally with other Roman citizens, dependent on the sovereign power, their sentiments of duty and honour were degraded by the loss of their former dignity; and being likewise deprived of the lucrative governments of provinces, to which they had annually succeeded by an elective rotation in the times of the republic, they endeavoured to compensate the reduction of their emoluments by an unbounded venality in the judicial decisions of the forum. Every source of national happiness and prosperity was by this means destroyed. The possession of property became precarious; industry, in all its branches, was effectually discouraged, and the amor patriae, which had formerly been the animating principle of the nation, was almost universally extinguished.

It is a circumstance corresponding to the general singularity of the present reign, that, of the few writers who flourished in it, and whose works have been transmitted to posterity, two ended their days by the order of the emperor, and the third, from indignation at his conduct. These unfortunate victims were Seneca, Petronius Arbiter, and Lucan.

Seneca was born about six years before the Christian aera, and gave early indication of uncommon talents. His father, who had come from Corduba to Rome, was a man of letters, particularly fond of declamation, in which he instructed his son, and placed him, for the acquisition of philosophy, under the most celebrated stoics of that age. Young Seneca, imbibing the precepts of the Pythagorean doctrine, religiously abstained from eating the flesh of animals, until Tiberius having threatened to punish some Jews and Egyptians, who abstained from certain meats, he was persuaded by his father to renounce the Pythagorean practice. Seneca displayed the talents of an eloquent speaker; but dreading the jealousy of Caligula, who aspired to the same excellence, he thought proper to abandon that pursuit, and apply himself towards suing for the honours and offices of the state. He accordingly obtained the place of quaestor, in which office incurring the imputation of a scandalous amour with Julia Livia, he removed from Rome, and was banished by the emperor Claudius to Corsica.

Upon the marriage of Claudius with Agrippina, Seneca was recalled from his exile, in which he had remained near eight years, and was appointed to superintend the education of Nero, now destined to become the successor to the throne. In the character of preceptor he appears to have acquitted himself with ability and credit; though he has been charged by his enemies with having initiated his pupil in those detestable vices which disgraced the reign of Nero. Could he have indeed been guilty of such immoral conduct, it is probable that he would not so easily have forfeited the favour of that emperor; and it is more reasonable to suppose, that his disapprobation of Nero's conduct was the real cause of that odium which soon after proved fatal to him. By the enemies whom distinguished merit and virtue never fail to excite at a profligate court, Seneca was accused of having maintained a criminal correspondence with Agrippina in the life-time of Claudius; but the chief author of this calumny was Suilius, who had been banished from Rome at the instance of Seneca. He was likewise charged with having amassed exorbitant riches, with having built magnificent houses, and formed beautiful gardens, during the four years in which he had acted as preceptor to Nero. This charge he considered as a prelude to his destruction; which to avoid, if possible, he requested of the emperor to accept of the riches and possessions which he had acquired in his situation at court, and to permit him to withdraw himself into a life of studious retirement. Nero, dissembling his secret intentions, refused this request; and Seneca, that he might obviate all cause of suspicion or offence, kept himself at home for some time, under the pretext of indisposition.

Upon the breaking out of the conspiracy of Piso, in which some of the principal senators were concerned, Natalis, the discoverer of the plot, mentioned Seneca's name, as an accessory. There is, however, no satisfactory evidence that Seneca had any knowledge of the plot. Piso, according to the declaration of Natalis, had complained that he never saw Seneca; and the latter had observed, in answer, that it was not conducive to their common interest to see each other often. Seneca likewise pleaded indisposition, and said that his own life depended upon the safety of Piso's person. Nero, however, glad of such an occasion of sacrificing the philosopher to his secret jealousy, sent him an order to destroy himself. When the messenger arrived with this mandate, Seneca was sitting at table, with his wife Paulina and two of his friends. He heard the message not only with philosophical firmness, but even with symptoms of joy, and observed, that such an honour might long have been expected from a man who had assassinated all his friends, and even murdered his own mother. The only request which he made, was, that he might be permitted to dispose of his possessions as he pleased; but this was refused him. Immediately turning himself to his friends, who were weeping at his melancholy fate, he said to them, that, since he could not leave them what he considered as his own property, he should leave at least his own life for an example; an innocence of conduct which they might imitate, and by which they might acquire immortal fame. He remonstrated with composure against their unavailing tears and lamentations, and asked them, whether they had not learnt better to sustain the shocks of fortune, and the violence of tyranny?

The emotions of his wife he endeavoured to allay with philosophical consolation; and when she expressed a resolution to die with him, he said, that he was glad to find his example imitated with so much fortitude. The veins of both were opened at the same time; but Nero's command extending only to Seneca, the life of Paulina was preserved; and, according to some authors, she was not displeased at being prevented from carrying her precipitate resolution into effect. Seneca's veins bleeding but slowly, an opportunity was offered him of displaying in his last moments a philosophical magnanimity similar to that of Socrates; and it appears that his conversation during this solemn period was maintained with dignified composure. To accelerate his lingering fate, he drank a dose of poison; but this producing no effect, he ordered his attendants to carry him into a warm bath, for the purpose of rendering the haemorrhage from his veins more copious. This expedient proving likewise ineffectual, and the soldiers who witnessed the execution of the emperor's order being clamorous for its accomplishment, he was removed into a stove, and suffocated by the steam. He underwent his fate on the 12th of April, in the sixty-fifth year of the Christian aera, and the fifty-third year of his age. His body was burnt, and his ashes deposited in a private manner, according to his will, which had been made during the period when he was in the highest degree of favour with Nero.

The writings of Seneca are numerous, and on various subjects. His first composition, addressed to Novacus, is on Anger, and continued through three books. After giving a lively description of this passion, the author discusses a variety of questions concerning it: he argues strongly against its utility, in contradiction to the peripatetics, and recommends its restraint, by many just and excellent considerations. This treatise may be regarded, in its general outlines, as a philosophical amplification of the passage in Horace:--

Ira furor brevis est: animum rege; qui, nisi paret, Imperat: hunc fraenis, hunc tu compesce catena. Epist. I. ii.

Anger's a fitful madness: rein thy mind, Subdue the tyrant, and in fetters bind, Or be thyself the slave.

The next treatise is on Consolation, addressed to his mother, Helvia, and was written during his exile. He there informs his mother that he bears his banishment with fortitude, and advises her to do the same. He observes, that, in respect to himself, change of place, poverty, ignominy, and contempt, are not real evils; that there may be two reasons for her anxiety on his account; first, that, by his absence, she is deprived of his protection; and in the next place, of the satisfaction arising from his company; on both which heads he suggests a variety of pertinent observations.

Prefixed to this treatise, are some epigrams written on the banishment of Seneca, but whether or not by himself, is uncertain.

Immediately subsequent to the preceding, is another treatise on Consolation, addressed to one of Claudius's freedmen, named Polybius, perhaps after the learned historian. In this tract, which is in several parts mutilated, the author endeavours to console Polybius for the loss of a brother who had lately died. The sentiments and admonitions are well suggested for the purpose; but they are intermixed with such fulsome encomiums on the imperial domestic, as degrade the dignity of the author, and can be ascribed to no other motive than that of endeavouring to procure a recall from his exile, through the interest of Polybius.

A fourth treatise on Consolation is addressed to Marcia, a respectable and opulent lady, the daughter of Cremutius Cordus, by whose death she was deeply affected. The author, besides many consolatory arguments, proposes for her imitation a number of examples, by attending to which she may be enabled to overcome a passion that is founded only in too great sensibility of mind. The subject is ingeniously prosecuted, not without the occasional mixture of some delicate flattery, suitable to the character of the correspondent.

These consolatory addresses are followed by a treatise on Providence, which evinces the author to have entertained the most just and philosophical sentiments on that subject. He infers the necessary existence of a Providence from the regularity and constancy observed in the government of the universe but his chief object is to show, why, upon the principle that a Providence exists, good men should be liable to evils. The enquiry is conducted with a variety of just observations, and great force of argument; by which the author vindicates the goodness and wisdom of the Almighty, in a strain of sentiment corresponding to the most approved suggestions of natural religion.

The next treatise, which is on Tranquillity of Mind, appears to have been written soon after his return from exile. There is a confusion in the arrangement of this tract; but it contains a variety of just observations, and may be regarded as a valuable production.

Then follows a discourse on the Constancy of a Wise Man. This has by some been considered as a part of the preceding treatise; but they are evidently distinct. It is one of the author's best productions, in regard both of sentiment and composition, and contains a fund of moral observations, suited to fortify the mind under the oppression of accidental calamities.

We next meet with a tract on Clemency, in two books, addressed to Nero. This appears to have been written in the beginning of the reign of Nero, on whom the author bestows some high encomiums, which, at that time, seem not to have been destitute of foundation. The discourse abounds with just observation, applicable to all ranks of men; and, if properly attended to by that infatuated emperor, might have prevented the perpetration of those acts of cruelty, which, with his other extravagancies, have rendered his name odious to posterity.

The discourse which succeeds is on the Shortness of Life, addressed to Paulinus. In this excellent treatise the author endeavours to show, that the complaint of the shortness of life is not founded in truth: that it is men who make life short, either by passing it in indolence, or otherwise improperly. He inveighs against indolence, luxury, and every unprofitable avocation; observing, that the best use of time is to apply it to the study of wisdom, by which life may be rendered sufficiently long.

Next follows a discourse on a Happy Life, addressed to Gallio. Seneca seems to have intended this as a vindication of himself, against those who calumniated him on account of his riches and manner of living. He maintained that a life can only be rendered happy by its conformity to the dictates of virtue, but that such a life is perfectly compatible with the possession of riches, where they happen to accrue. The author pleads his own cause with great ability, as well as justness of argument. His vindication is in many parts highly beautiful, and accompanied with admirable sentiments respecting the moral obligations to a virtuous life. The conclusion of this discourse bears no similarity, in point of composition, to the preceding parts, and is evidently spurious.

The preceding discourse is followed by one upon the Retirement of a Wise Man. The beginning of this tract is wanting; but in the sequel the author discusses a question which was much agitated amongst the Stoics and Epicureans, viz., whether a wise man ought to concern himself with the affairs of the public. Both these sects of philosophers maintained that a life of retirement was most suitable to a wise man, but they differed with respect to the circumstances in which it might be proper to deviate from this conduct; one party considering the deviation as prudent, when there existed a just motive for such conduct, and the other, when there was no forcible reason against it. Seneca regards both these opinions as founded upon principles inadequate to the advancement both of public and private happiness, which ought ever to be the ultimate object of moral speculation.

The last of the author's discourses, addressed to Aebucius, is on Benefits, and continued through seven books. He begins with lamenting the frequency of ingratitude amongst mankind, a vice which he severely censures. After some preliminary considerations respecting the nature of benefits, he proceeds to show in what manner, and on whom, they ought to be conferred. The greater part of these books is employed on the solution of abstract questions relative to benefits, in the manner of Chrysippus; where the author states explicitly the arguments on both sides, and from the full consideration of them, deduces rational conclusions.

The Epistles of Seneca consist of one hundred and twenty-four, all on moral subjects. His Natural Questions extend through seven books, in which he has collected the hypotheses of Aristotle and other ancient writers. These are followed by a whimsical effusion on the death of Caligula. The remainder of his works comprises seven Persuasive Discourses, five books of Controversies, and ten books containing Extracts of Declamations.

From the multiplicity of Seneca's productions, it is evident, that, notwithstanding the luxurious life he is said to have led, he was greatly devoted to literature, a propensity which, it is probable, was confirmed by his banishment during almost eight years in the island of Corsica, where he was in a great degree secluded from every other resource of amusement to a cultivated mind. But with whatever splendour Seneca's domestic economy may have been supported, it seems highly improbable that he indulged himself in luxurious enjoyment to any vicious excess. His situation at the Roman court, being honourable and important, could not fail of being likewise advantageous, not only from the imperial profusion common at that time, but from many contingent emoluments which his extensive interest and patronage would naturally afford him. He was born of a respectable rank, lived in habits of familiar intercourse with persons of the first distinction, and if, in the course of his attendance upon Nero, he had acquired a large fortune, no blame could justly attach to his conduct in maintaining an elegant hospitality. The imputation of luxury was thrown upon him from two quarters, viz, by the dissolute companions of Nero, to whom the mention of such an example served as an apology for their own extreme dissipation; and by those who envied him for the affluence and dignity which he had acquired. The charge, however, is supported only by vague assertion, and is discredited by every consideration which ought to have weight in determining the reality of human characters. It seems totally inconsistent with his habits of literary industry, with the virtuous sentiments which he every where strenuously maintains, and the esteem with which he was regarded by a numerous acquaintance, as a philosopher and a moralist.

The writings of Seneca have been traduced almost equally with his manner of living, though in both he has a claim to indulgence, from the fashion of the times. He is more studious of minute embellishments in style than the writers of the Augustan age; and the didactic strain, in which he mostly prosecutes his subjects, has a tendency to render him sententious; but the expression of his thoughts is neither enfeebled by decoration, nor involved in obscurity by conciseness. He is not more rich in artificial ornament than in moral admonition. Seneca has been charged with depreciating former writers, to render himself more conspicuous; a charge which, so far as appears from his writings, is founded rather in negative than positive testimony. He has not endeavoured to establish his fame by any affectation of singularity in doctrine; and while he passes over in silence the names of illustrious authors, he avails himself with judgment of the most valuable stores with which they had enriched philosophy. On the whole, he is an author whose principles may be adopted not only with safety, but great advantage; and his writings merit a degree of consideration, superior to what they have hitherto ever enjoyed in the literary world.

Seneca, besides his prose works, was the author of some tragedies. The Medea, the Troas, and the Hippolytus, are ascribed to him. His father is said to have written the Hercules Furens, Thyestes, Agamemnon, and Hercules Oetaeus. The three remaining tragedies, the Thebais, Oedipus, and Octavia, usually published in the same collection with the seven preceding, are supposed to be the productions of other authors, but of whom, is uncertain. These several pieces are written in a neat style; the plots and characters are conducted with an attention to probability and nature: but none of them is so forcible, in point of tragical distress, as to excite in the reader any great degree of emotion.----

Petronius was a Roman knight, and apparently of considerable fortune. In his youth he seems to have given great application to polite literature, in which he acquired a justness of taste, as well as an elegance of composition. Early initiated in the gaieties of fashionable life, he contracted a habit of voluptuousness which rendered him an accommodating companion to the dissipated and the luxurious. The court of Claudius, entirely governed for some time by Messalina, was then the residence of pleasure; and here Petronius failed not of making a conspicuous appearance. More delicate, however, than sensual, he rather joined in the dissipation, than indulged in the vices of the palace. To interrupt a course of life too uniform to afford him perpetual satisfaction, he accepted of the proconsulship of Bithynia, and went to that province, where he discharged the duties of his office with great credit. Upon his return to Rome,

Nero, who had succeeded Claudius, made him consul, in recompense of his services. This new dignity, by giving him frequent and easy access to the emperor, created an intimacy between them, which was increased to friendship and esteem on the side of Nero, by the elegant entertainments often given him by Petronius. In a short time, this gay voluptuary became so much a favourite at court, that nothing was agreeable but what was approved by Petronius and the authority which he acquired, by being umpire in whatever related to the economy of gay dissipation, procured him the title of Arbiter elegantiarum. Things continued in this state whilst the emperor kept within the bounds of moderation; and Petronius acted as intendant of his pleasures, ordering him shows, games, comedies, music, feats, and all that could contribute to make the hours of relaxation pass agreeably; seasoning, at the same time, the innocent delights which he procured for the emperor with every possible charm, to prevent him from seeking after such as might prove pernicious both to morals and the republic. Nero, however, giving way to his own disposition, which was naturally vicious, at length changed his conduct, not only in regard to the government of the empire, but of himself and listening to other counsels than those of Petronius, gave the entire reins to his passions, which afterwards plunged him in ruin. The emperor's new favourite was Tigellinus, a man of the most profligate morals, who omitted nothing that could gratify the inordinate appetites of his prince, at the expense of all decency and virtue. During this period, Petronius gave vent to his indignation, in the satire transmitted under his name by the title of Satyricon. But his total retirement from court did not secure him from the artifices of Tigellinus, who laboured with all his power to destroy the man whom he had industriously supplanted in the emperor's favour. With this view he insinuated to Nero, that Petronius was too intimately connected with Scevinus not to be engaged in Piso's conspiracy; and, to support his calumny, caused the emperor to be present at the examination of one of Petronius's slaves, whom he had secretly suborned to swear against his master. After this transaction, to deprive Petronius of all means of justifying himself, they threw into prison the greatest part of his domestics. Nero embraced with joy the opportunity of removing a man, to whom he knew the present manners of the court were utterly obnoxious, and he soon after issued orders for arresting Petronius. As it required, however, some time to deliberate whether they should put a person of his consideration to death, without more evident proofs of the charges preferred against him, such was his disgust at living in the power of so detestable and capricious a tyrant, that he resolved to die. For this purpose, making choice of the same expedient which had been adopted by Seneca, he caused his veins to be opened, but he closed them again, for a little time, that he might enjoy the conversation of his friends, who came to see him in his last moments. He desired them, it is said, to entertain him, not with discourses on the immortality of the soul, or the consolation of philosophy, but with agreeable tales and poetic gallantries. Disdaining to imitate the servility of those who, dying by the orders of Nero, yet made him their heir, and filled their wills with encomiums on the tyrant and his favourites, he broke to pieces a goblet of precious stones, out of which he had commonly drank, that Nero, who he knew would seize upon it after his death, might not have the pleasure of using it. As the only present suitable to such a prince, he sent him, under a sealed cover, his Satyricon, written purposely against him;

and then broke his signet, that it might not, after his death, become the means of accusation against the person in whose custody it should be found.

The Satyricon of Petronius is one of the most curious productions in the Latin language. Novel in its nature, and without any parallel in the works of antiquity, some have imagined it to be a spurious composition, fabricated about the time of the revival of learning in Europe. This conjecture, however, is not more destitute of support, than repugnant to the most circumstantial evidence in favour of its authenticity. Others, admitting the work to be a production of the age of Nero, have questioned the design with which it was written, and have consequently imputed to the author a most immoral intention. Some of the scenes, incidents, and characters, are of so extraordinary a nature, that the description of them, without a particular application, must have been regarded as extremely whimsical, and the work, notwithstanding its ingenuity, has been doomed to perpetual oblivion: but history justifies the belief, that in the court of Nero, the extravagancies mentioned by Petronius were realized to a degree which authenticates the representation given of them. The inimitable character of Trimalchio, which exhibits a person sunk in the most debauched effeminacy, was drawn for Nero; and we are assured, that there were formerly medals of that emperor, with these words, C. Nero August. Imp., and on the reverse, Trimalchio. The various characters are well discriminated, and supported with admirable propriety. Never was such licentiousness of description united to such delicacy of colouring. The force of the satire consists not in poignancy of sentiment, but in the ridicule which arises from the whimsical, but characteristic and faithful exhibition of the objects introduced. That Nero was struck with the justness of the representation, is evident from the displeasure which he showed, at finding Petronius so well acquainted with his infamous excesses. After levelling his suspicion on all who could possibly have betrayed him, he at last fixed on a senator's wife, named Silia, who bore a part in his revels, and was an intimate friend of Petronius upon which she was immediately sent into banishment. Amongst the miscellaneous materials in this work, are some pieces of poetry, written in an elegant taste. A poem on the civil war between Caesar and Pompey, is beautiful and animated.

Though the Muses appear to have been mostly in a quiescent state from the time of Augustus, we find from Petronius Arbiter, who exhibits the manners of the capital during the reign of Nero, that poetry still continued to be a favourite pursuit amongst the Romans, and one to which, indeed, they seem to have had a national propensity.

--------Ecce inter pocula quaerunt Romulidae saturi, quid dia poemata narrent.--Persius, Sat. i. 30.

----Nay, more! Our nobles, gorged, and swilled with wine, Call o'er the banquet for a lay divine!--Gifford.

It was cultivated as a kind of fashionable exercise, in short and desultory attempts, in which the chief ambition was to produce verses extempore. They were publicly recited by their authors with great ostentation; and a favourable verdict from an audience, however partial, and frequently obtained either by intrigue or bribery, was construed by those frivolous pretenders into a real adjudication of poetical fame.

The custom of publicly reciting poetical compositions, with the view of obtaining the opinion of the hearers concerning them, and for which purpose Augustus had built the Temple of Apollo, was well calculated for the improvement of taste and judgment, as well as the excitement of emulation; but, conducted as it now was, it led to a general degradation of poetry. Barbarism in language, and a corruption of taste, were the natural consequences of this practice, while the judgment of the multitude was either blind or venal, and while public approbation sanctioned the crudities of hasty composition. There arose, however, in this period, some candidates for the bays, who carried their efforts beyond the narrow limits which custom and inadequate genius prescribed to the poetical exertions of their contemporaries. Amongst these were Lucan and Persius.----

Lucan was the son of Annaeus Mela, the brother of Seneca, the philosopher. He was born at Corduba, the original residence of the family, but came early to Rome, where his promising talents, and the patronage of his uncle, recommended him to the favour of Nero; by whom he was raised to the dignity of an augur and quaestor before he had attained the usual age. Prompted by the desire of displaying his political abilities, he had the imprudence to engage in a competition with his imperial patron. The subject chosen by Nero was the tragical fate of Niobe; and that of Lucan was Orpheus. The ease with which the latter obtained the victory in the contest, excited the jealousy of the emperor, who resolved upon depressing his rising genius. With this view, he exposed him daily to the mortification of fresh insults, until at last the poet's resentment was so much provoked, that he entered into the conspiracy of Piso for cutting off the tyrant. The plot being discovered, there remained for the unfortunate Lucan no hope of pardon: and choosing the same mode of death which was employed by his uncle, he had his veins opened, while he sat in a warm bath, and expired in pronouncing with great emphasis the following lines in his Pharsalia:--

Scinditur avulsus; nec sicut vulnere sanguis Emicuit lentus: ruptis cadit undique venis; Discursusque animae diversa in membra meantis Interceptus aquis, nullius, vita perempti Est tanta dimissa via.--Lib. iii. 638.


----Asunder flies the man. No single wound the gaping rupture seems, Where trickling crimson flows in tender streams; But from an opening horrible and wide A thousand vessels pour the bursting tide; At once the winding channel's course was broke, Where wandering life her mazy journey took.--Rowe.


Some authors have said that he betrayed pusillanimity at the hour of death; and that, to save himself from punishment, he accused his mother of being involved in the conspiracy. This circumstance, however, is not mentioned by other writers, who relate, on the contrary, that he died with philosophical fortitude. He was then only in the twenty-sixth year of his age.


Lucan had scarcely reached the age of puberty when he wrote a poem on the contest between Hector and Achilles. He also composed in his youth a poem on the burning of Rome; but his only surviving work is the Pharsalia, written on the civil war between Caesar and Pompey. This poem, consisting of ten books, is unfinished, and its character has been more depreciated than that of any other production of antiquity. In the plan of the poem, the author prosecutes the different events in the civil war, beginning his narrative at the passage of the Rubicon by Caesar. He invokes not the muses, nor engages any gods in the dispute; but endeavours to support an epic dignity by vigour of sentiment, and splendour of description. The horrors of civil war, and the importance of a contest which was to determine the fate of Rome and the empire of the world, are displayed with variety of colouring, and great energy of expression. In the description of scenes, and the recital of heroic actions, the author discovers a strong and lively imagination; while, in those parts of the work which are addressed either to the understanding or the passions, he is bold, figurative, and animated. Indulging too much in amplification, he is apt to tire with prolixity; but in all his excursions he is ardent, elevated, impressive, and often brilliant. His versification has not the smoothness which we admire in the compositions of Virgil, and his language is often involved in the intricacies of technical construction: but with all his defects, his beauties are numerous; and he discovers a greater degree of merit than is commonly found in the productions of a poet of twenty-six years of age, at which time he died.----

Persius was born at Volaterrae, of an equestrian family, about the beginning of the Christian aera. His father dying when he was six years old, he was left to the care of his mother, for whom and for his sisters he expresses the warmest affection. At the age of twelve he came to Rome, where, after attending a course of grammar and rhetoric under the respective masters of those branches of education, he placed himself under the tuition of Annaeus Cornutus, a celebrated stoic philosopher of that time. There subsisted between him and this preceptor so great a friendship, that at his death, which happened in the twenty-ninth year of his age, he bequeathed to Cornutus a handsome sum of money, and his library. The latter, however, accepting only the books, left the money to Persius's sisters.

Priscian, Quintilian, and other ancient writers, spear of Persius's satires as consisting of a book without any division. They have since, however, been generally divided into six different satires, but by some only into five. The subjects of these compositions are, the vanity of the poets in his time; the backwardness of youth to the cultivation of moral science; ignorance and temerity in political administration, chiefly in allusion to the government of Nero: the fifth satire is employed in evincing that the wise man also is free; in discussing which point, the author adopts the observations used by Horace on the same subject. The last satire of Persius is directed against avarice. In the fifth, we meet with a beautiful address to Cornutus, whom the author celebrates for his amiable virtues, and peculiar talents for teaching. The following lines, at the same time that they show how diligently the preceptor and his pupil were employed through the whole day in the cultivation of moral science, afford a more agreeable picture of domestic comfort and philosophical conviviality, than might be expected in the family of a rigid stoic:

Tecum etenim longos memini consumere soles, Et tecum primas epulis decerpere noctes.
Unum opus, et requiem pariter disponimus ambo: Atque verecunda laxamus feria mensa.--Sat. v.

Can I forget how many a summer's day, Spent in your converse, stole, unmarked, away? Or how, while listening with increased delight, I snatched from feasts the earlier hours of night?--Gifford.

The satires of Persius are written in a free, expostulatory, and argumentative manner; possessing the same justness of sentiment as those of Horace, but exerted in the way of derision, and not with the admirable raillery of that facetious author. They are regarded by many as obscure; but this imputation arises more from unacquaintance with the characters and manners to which the author alludes, than from any peculiarity either in his language or composition. His versification is harmonious; and we have only to remark, in addition to similar examples in other Latin writers, that, though Persius is acknowledged to have been both virtuous and modest, there are in the fourth satire a few passages which cannot decently admit of being translated. Such was the freedom of the Romans, in the use of some expressions, which just refinement has now exploded.--

Another poet, in this period, was Fabricius Veiento, who wrote a severe satire against the priests of his time; as also one against the senators, for corruption in their judicial capacity. Nothing remains of either of those productions; but, for the latter, the author was banished by Nero.

There now likewise flourished a lyric poet, Caesius Bassus, to whom Persius has addressed his sixth satire. He is said to have been, next to Horace, the best lyric poet among the Romans; but of his various compositions, only a few inconsiderable fragments are preserved.

To the two poets now mentioned must be added Pomponius Secundus, a man of distinguished rank in the army, and who obtained the honour of a triumph for a victory over a tribe of barbarians in Germany. He wrote several tragedies, which in the judgment of Quintilian, were beautiful compositions.

### Bibliography

There is a wealth of ancient sources that interested readers can consult to learn more about Nero (though annotated versions, given the controversial nature of the material, are recommended): readers should refer to the works of Cassius Dio, Tacitus, Plutarch, Josephus, and Suetonius. For a more modern take, see Miriam Griffin's *Nero: The End of a Dynasty*, Edward Champlin's *Nero*, and David Shotter's *Nero Caesar Augustus: Emperor of Rome*.

Made in the USA
Lexington, KY
11 November 2018